Understand Stalin's

Teach Yourself®

Understand Stalin's Russia

David Evans

Hodder Education

338 Euston Road, London NW1 3BH.

Hodder Education is an Hachette UK company

First published in UK 2005 by Hodder Education

This edition published 2012.

Hachette UK's policy is to use papers that are natural, renewable and recyclable products and made from wood grown in sustainable forests. The logging and manufacturing processes are expected to conform to the environmental regulations of the country of origin.

www.hoddereducation.co.uk

Typeset by Cenveo Publisher Services.

Printed and bound by CPI Group (UK) Ltd, Croydon, CR0 4YY.

Contents

Russia at the time of Stalin's birth

This chapter will cover:
- *the Djugashvili family and the birth of Josif Stalin*
- *the extent of Russia and the diversity of the Russian people*
- *the rule of the Romanov dynasty of tsars*
- *the condition of the Russian people*
- *the early revolutionaries.*

> *Russian society is similar to a colony of bees in which royalty is a natural necessity. Just as the colony of bees would cease to exist without a queen, so too would Russian society cease to exist without the Tsar.*
>
> August von Haxthausen, 1792–1866

The Djugashvili family

On 17 May 1874, 24-year-old Vissarion Djugashvili married 16-year-old Ekaterina Geladze in Gori, a small town at the mouth of the River Kura in Georgia. Vissarion, or Beso as he was known, came from a family of former serfs and was a shoemaker by trade. He drank heavily and was a morose, evil-tempered man who easily turned to violence. Of peasant stock, his young wife Ekaterina, or Keke as family and friends called her, was hard working. The family was poor and Keke took in laundry and repaired clothes in order to earn extra money. They lived in a run-down house on the edge of the village that remains to this day and is now a tourist attraction. Their first two sons, Mikhail and Georgi, died in infancy and when Keke became pregnant for the third time, she prayed that her unborn child would survive and even promised that he would become a priest.

Josif Vissarionovich Djugashvili was born on 21 December 1879. His mother, who doted on her baby son, called him Soso. In later life he was to take the name Stalin, 'Man of Steel', and become one of the most evil tyrants in history. He was to lead his country into a period described by some historians as 'years of impenetrable darkness'. In many ways, his monstrous crimes were to exceed even those of Adolf Hitler!

In order to appreciate the situation in Russia at the time of Stalin's birth and the influences that dictated his life, it is necessary to be aware of the enormity of the country, its diversity, its system of government and the condition of the Russian people.

Imperial Russia

THE GEOGRAPHY

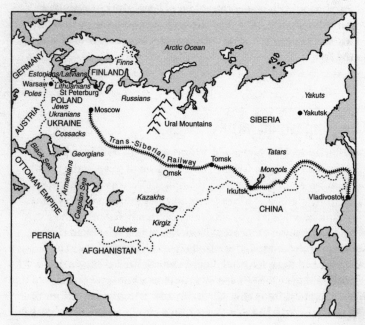

Figure 1.1 Imperial Russia in the mid-nineteenth century.

Imperial Russia was by far the largest country in the world and covered one-eighth of the Earth's inhabited area. Its vast land mass extended over 9,600 kilometres (5,966 miles) from eastern Europe across the Ural Mountains into Asia to finally reach the Bering Straits at the most eastern point of Siberia. From north to south, Russian territory stretched 3,300 kilometres (2,051 miles) from the Arctic Circle to the frontiers of Persia (present day Iran), Nepal and Mongolia. The Ural Mountains, running 2,200 kilometres (1,367 miles) from north to south, form a boundary separating Russia-in-Europe from Russia-in-Asia. The country's terrain is diverse. In the north, where the winters are harsh and the lowest temperature ever recorded was −94 degrees centigrade, the landscape is frozen tundra of treeless plain. To the south lies the tiagra, a large forested area of coniferous spruce. Further south lies the steppes, a broad band of grassy plains that offers the most favourable conditions for settlement and agriculture. South of the steppes, the land becomes semi-desert. In contrast, a small area along the Black Sea coast is sub-tropical.

Russia was also a country of 120,000 rivers and numerous lakes. The longest rivers include the Volga, Dnepr, Don, Ob, Yenisey, Lena and Amur. The largest lake is the Caspian Sea. Approximately two-thirds of Russia's border is bound by water. Although the country possessed immense mineral wealth, by the mid-nineteenth century it remained undeveloped.

THE PEOPLE

With a total population of some 69 million, Imperial Russia was made up of peoples of many different cultures and religions.

Note that Stalin was a Georgian, a people that only represented one per cent of the Russian population. It was also his native tongue and throughout his life he spoke Russian with a strong Georgian accent.

With a population of half a million, the capital of Imperial Russia was Saint Petersburg. Other large towns included Moscow, Warsaw, Kharkov, Kiev and Odessa whilst in remote Siberia, Omsk, Tomsk, Yakutsk and Vladivostok were the only towns of any size. Most ethnic Russians were Christian and belonged to the Russian Orthodox Church but there were also some 25 million Muslims and 5 million Jews.

Table 1.1   The peoples of imperial Russia (based on the census of 1897)

Nationality	Total number	As a percentage of the total population
Great Russians	55,650,000	44.3
Ukrainians	22,400,000	17.8
Poles	7,900,000	6.3
White Russians	5,900,000	4.7
Jews	5,000,000	4.0
Kirghiz	4,000,000	3.2
Tartars	3,700,000	3.0
Finns	2,500,000	2.0
Germans	1,800,000	1.4
Lithuanians	1,650,000	1.4
Letts	1,400,000	1.1
Georgians	1,350,000	1.0
Armenians	1,150,000	0.9
Romanians	1,100,000	0.9
Caucasians	1,000,000	0.8
Estonians	1,000,000	0.8
Iranians	1,000,000	0.8
Mongols	500,000	0.4
Other Turkish people	5,750,000	4.7
Others	200,000	0.2

THE TSAR AND THE RUSSIAN NOBILITY

Tsars of the House of Romanov had ruled Russia since 1613. As with the German Kaiser, the word tsar (which is sometimes spelt czar or tsar) is derived from the Latin Caesar and means an absolute monarch or dictator. In 1879, the year of Stalin's birth, Russia was ruled by Tsar Alexander II. A plump and amiable man, he had carried out a number of education, local government and military reforms and by freeing the serfs (see below) had earned himself the title 'Liberator

Tsar'. Nevertheless, in 1881 terrorists assassinated him. His successor, Alexander III, was a very different sort of man. He reversed many of his father's reforms and revived old methods of repression. It was during his reign that Russia began to industrialize and this created urban communities of industrial workers who suffered wretched working and living conditions. He died in 1894 and was succeeded by his son Nicholas II. As we shall see, Nicholas was to be the last of the Russian tsars. Nicholas was a weak man with no real sympathy with the liberal aspirations of the Russian people. His wife, formerly Princess Alexandra of Hesse-Darmstadt, was the granddaughter of Britain's Queen Victoria.

The tsars were autocrats who ruled by themselves without consulting a parliament. They appointed ministers who were little more than obedient yes-men. What advice they sought came from court favourites who were drawn from the nobility and were mainly wealthy landowners. It became necessary for the tsars to run the country by employing a vast number of civil servants, the most senior of which became very powerful. Many practised nepotism by favouring their own relations and appointing them to senior positions. Most important, since it was his responsibility to ensure that the Russian people remained obedient to the tsar, was the Minister of the Interior. He was head of the much-feared secret police, the Third Section or *Okhrana*, as it became known. It would not tolerate any criticism, censored the press and aimed to seek out those opposed to the tsar. The *Okhrana* was responsible for sending thousands of innocent Russians into exile in Siberia.

Within the Russian social structure, the most privileged were the nobility. The majority were hereditary and they formed a ruling elite. Apart from controlling the lives of their serfs, many lived lives of great extravagance and paid no taxes. The middle class, such as it was, comprised professional people such as doctors, teachers and government officials. It also included businessmen such as tradesmen and shopkeepers. A few became quite wealthy but they possessed no political power and did not share the privileges of the nobility and Church.

THE RUSSIAN ORTHODOX CHURCH AND THE PRIESTHOOD

In addition to the nobility, the Russian Orthodox Church was another pillar of the establishment that supported the autocratic rule of the tsar. Whilst the tsar was the head of the Church, a committee, the Holy Synod, controlled it. The Holy Synod was headed by one of the tsar's ministers who acted as overseer or procurator. The bishops and other high-ranking clergy kept a close watch on local priests to ensure that they showed due respect for the tsar and his autocratic rule and even went as far as to censor their sermons. The Church provided most of the schools but these only catered for the needs of the wealthy. The tsarist regime and the Church did not favour providing education for the masses since this might cause people to demand change. The priests made their living from church collections made in money or in kind made on saints and other holy days and the fees they charged for marriage and funeral services. The peasantry, who considered them idle and parasitical, despised them. As one critic said, 'The priest takes from both the living and the dead'.

THE RUSSIAN PEASANTRY

Most Russians were peasants who struggled to make a living from their smallholdings. Prior to 1861, the majority had been serfs, a near slave status, which meant they were tied to the land on which they lived and worked and were, to all intents and purposes, the property of their landlords. In 1861, the situation changed when Tsar Alexander II passed a law that emancipated the serfs and made them free men. In a great many instances their position worsened since they had to buy their land and ended up with crippling burdens of debt. They and their families lived in appalling conditions. Apart from the occasional mining of coal, copper and precious metals and the manufacture of iron products, there was little industry. Like the landlords in the countryside, the few industrialists that existed were drawn from the Russian nobility. Their workmen worked excessively long hours for low and irregular wages and lived in slum urban conditions. The poet Ivan Krylov summed up the position of the downtrodden peasants and urban workers and he included a warning:

> *We are they,*
> *Who digging deep beneath the light of day,*
> *Keep you alive – or do the leaves not know? –*
> *The roots of that same tree on which yourselves you grow*
> *Then flaunt, the summer through,*
> *And yet this difference between us keep in view!*
> *When spring returns again, new leaves wave hither, thither,*
> *But if but once the roots should wither,*
> *The tree is gone, and so are you.*

OPPOSITION AND THE GROWTH OF TERROR

It was to be expected that miserable working and living conditions and the injustices imposed by tsarist autocratic rule would lead to the growth of opposition. Some middle class intellectuals, and even a few from noble families, held liberal views and favoured change. The poet Alexander Pushkin observed, 'God, what a sad country Russia is,' whilst Leo Tolstoy used his novels to highlight the injustices and openly sympathized with the plight of the peasants.

As early as 1825, conspirators had tried to remove the tsar when a group of army officers in St Petersburg plotted an uprising. The Decembrists, as they were called, were betrayed by police spies and their leaders executed. Amongst the more idealistic Russian intellectuals were those who wished to stir the peasant masses into popular revolt in order to overthrow the tsarist regime and change the political system. These Populists, or Narodniks as they were called, gained little support by 'going to the people' but attracted the attention of the tsar's secret police and thousands were arrested and sent into exile in Siberia. They next set up a terrorist organization, the People's Will, and condemned the tsar to death. After several failed attempts, in 1881 Alexander II was assassinated when a bomb was thrown at his carriage.

Few men have had such an influence over the political destiny as the German-born Karl Marx (1818–83). In his Communist Manifesto written jointly in 1848 with his close associate Friedrich Engels, he called on the oppressed working people of the world, the proletariat, to unite in a class war against those who were exploiting them, the landowners and capitalists. He wrote:

> **Let the ruling classes tremble at a communist revolution. The proletarians have nothing to lose but their chains. They have a world to win. Workers of the world unite.**

His *Das Kapital*, published in 1867, was a critical examination of the capitalist system and a statement of his own economic and social theories. Marxist ideas first spread to Russia in the 1880s and at a secret meeting in 1898, a Marxist Party, the Social Democratic Labour Party was formed with Vladimir Ulyanov (1870–1924), better known to the world as Lenin, as its leader.

...and back to the Djugashvili family

As a child, the young Josif Djugashvili was regularly beaten by his father, suffered ill health and was prone to accidents. Although afterwards his face remained badly scarred by pockmarks, he survived smallpox but after being knocked down by a cart suffered blood poisoning that caused his arm to wither and become deformed. When the family moved to Tbilisi, Keke urged her husband to allow their son to become a priest but Beso would have none of it and, instead, Josif was made to leave school and become an apprentice shoemaker. In 1890, Beso died after being knifed in a brawl and was buried in a pauper's grave. The death of his father meant that Josif could return to his studies. At school, he was teased because of his Georgian accent and poverty and he grew to resent the fact that lessons were taught in Russian and not in his native Georgian. In 1894 it seemed that he was about to fulfil his mother's wish when he won a scholarship to a seminary in Tbilisi. A clean-cut youth, he worked hard at his studies but found the oppressive regime imposed by the priests hard to tolerate. During his period at the seminary, he first became acquainted with the works of Charles Darwin, Karl Marx and Lenin. This brought about a profound change in his outlook and he joined a Georgian revolutionary group, *Mesame Dasi* or Third Group, and took part in demonstrations. These activities led to his expulsion from the seminary. It was during this period of his life that he became aware of class differences and grew to hate those who were better off than him. He became an atheist and began associating with Georgian nationalist groups such as the *Mesame Dasi*. However, as time passed, he became less a Georgian patriot and more a Marxist.

In 1904, Josif Djugashvili married Yeketerina Svanidze, a young peasant girl. They had a son, Yakov, but two years later Yeketerina died of tuberculosis. Her distraught husband said to a friend, 'She was the only creature who softened my heart. She is dead and with her have died any feelings of tenderness I had for humanity.' Afterwards, he devoted himself increasingly to politics and the cause of revolution. The year 1905 was to prove a turning point in his life for it was during that year that he first met Lenin in Tammerfors in Finland. Infatuated by the man, he became an admirer and staunch supporter. Afterwards he returned to his native Georgia and there took the title Koba, after a legendary local folk hero. In order to raise funds for the party, he engaged in acts of terrorism that included murder, robbery, blackmail and protection rackets. He also assisted in the publication of a revolutionary newspaper, *Mnatobi*, 'The Torch'. Under Lenin's influence, he abandoned terrorism and instead devoted his time to writing and distributing leaflets at workers' gatherings. He took pride in the fact that locally he was referred to as 'The Lenin of the Caucasus'. His various activities soon attracted the attention of the police and in 1902, as an active member of a group of Georgian Marxists, he was arrested for the first time. This meant that between 1901 and 1917, he spent most of his time in prison or living in exile. During these years he used many aliases but the one that stuck was Stalin – 'Man of Steel'.

Josif Stalin
Source: © Library of Congress Prints and Photographs Division Washington.

2

Towards revolution

This chapter will cover:
- *Russia's political parties and revolutionary groups*
- *the reasons why the Romanovs were able to survive the Dumas*
- *Russia's involvement in the First World War and its consequences*
- *the revolutions of 1917*
- *the failure of the Provisional Government.*

> *Society as a whole is more and more splitting up into two hostile camps, into two great classes directly facing each other – the bourgeoisie and the proletariat.*
>
> *The Communist Manifesto*, 1848

The political scene – the struggle to win the support of the working classes

Thanks to the efforts of Sergius Witte, the Russian Minister of Finance, the industrial development of the country began to gather momentum. Foreign investment helped to finance the development of heavy industry, the railway network was expanded and tariffs introduced to protect Russia's fledgling industries. The prestigious Trans-Siberian Railway, which was started in 1891, was completed in 1905 and linked St Petersburg with the military outpost and headquarters of the Russian Fleet, Vladivostock on the distant Pacific coast. Unfortunately, this new industrial prosperity did nothing to alleviate the suffering of the Russian masses and, in fact, made it worse. In the towns, the urban factory workers shared the wretchedness of their kinsfolk in the countryside. Extreme poverty as evident in the working and living conditions of the Russian people together with heavy taxation, high rents, indebtedness and unemployment affected all and this encouraged the growth of radical political parties that promised relief and reform. Some sought to bring about change and constitutional means but others were less patient.

The Social Democratic Labour Party, founded in 1898 at Minsk, was Marxist and set out to win the support of the distressed urban workers. Hounded by the tsar's secret police, in 1903 the Party was forced to hold its Second Congress in Tottenham Court Road in London. There differences arose between the leaders, Lenin and Georgi Plekhanov, and the delegates quarrelled bitterly. Lenin favoured a small, close knit and disciplined party dedicated to bringing about a revolution by any means; Plekhanov, on the other hand wanted a party based on a much broader membership that included those who were only mildly sympathetic to the movement. He was also opposed to the use of violence and terrorism. In the end, Lenin won the support of most of the delegates and became the leader of the larger group, the Bolsheviks, taken from the Russian word *Bolshinstvo*, which means majority. The remainder, known as the Mensheviks, from the Russian *Menshinstvo*, meaning minority, continued to support Plekhanov. Both groups continued to call themselves Social Democrats until they finally split in 1912.

Other political parties included the Social Revolutionary Party led by Victor Chernov and the Constitutional Democratic Party or Kadets. The Social Revolutionaries were largely supported by the peasants and, being more inclined to terrorist activities, were even more feared than the Bolsheviks! The Kadets were liberals who supported moderate policies of reform and sought greater freedom for the individual.

Tsarist reaction to the threat of revolution

Naturally Tsar Nicholas II was alarmed by the growth of revolutionary movements within his country and appointed Ministers of the Interior such as Konstantin Pobedonostev and Vyacheslav Plevhe to take the necessary repressive measures to deal with them. Pobedonostev, a firm supporter of absolute monarchy, was known as the 'Grand Inquisitor' whilst Plevhe, if anything was even more determined to uphold authoritarian principles. A clever but ruthless man, he mercilessly persecuted Russian Jews and organized their massacre in a series of bloody pogroms. He also, as part of a programme of 'Russification', tried to impose the Russian language and customs on Poles, Finns, Armenians and other minorities living within the Empire. Cunningly, he set up the Assembly of Russian Working Men, which purported to encourage free expression and settle grievances but in reality it was used to spy on troublemakers and ensure they were known to the secret police. In 1904, Plehve was assassinated and his place taken by the more liberal minded Prince Svyatopolk Mirsky.

The war with Japan and the revolution of 1904

Before his murder, Plehve had pressed Nicholas to embark on a small, victorious war that, so he claimed, 'would stop the revolutionary tide'. The Tsar was impressed by the idea that a spectacular military victory abroad might bring glory to Russia, increase his popularity with his people and ease the pressure for reform. In 1904, since relations with Japan were at a low ebb, the Tsar decided to match the military and naval might of Russia against a small and presumably weak enemy. From a Russian viewpoint, this proved an unmitigated disaster.

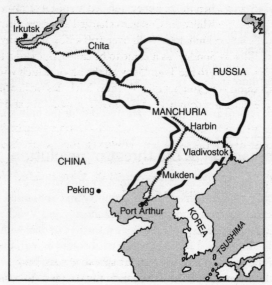

Figure 2.1 The Russo-Japanese War of 1904–5.

The Japanese first defeated the Russian fleet based at Port Arthur and later, at the Battle of Tsushima, destroyed the Russian Baltic fleet sent to the Far East to replace it. The battle lasted less than an hour! On land, the Tsar's armies fared little better. Although they fought bravely enough, the Russian soldiers were led by incompetent generals, Anatoli Stossel and Alexaei Kuropatin, and suffered heavy defeats both along the Yalu River and at the Battle of Mukden. Humiliated on land and at sea, the Tsar was forced to agree to accept the offer of the American President, Theodore Roosevelt, to mediate between the warring powers and peace was restored by the Treaty of Portsmouth (New Hampshire).

The Tsar's scheme to win popularity had ended in disaster and as news of the defeats filtered through to the Russian people, their despair turned to anger. Workers in the towns and cities took to the streets and rioted whilst there was disorder in the countryside. On 22 January 1905, Father Peter Gapon led a peaceful procession to the tsar's Winter Palace in St Petersburg. The previous day he had sent a letter to the Tsar, 'The people believe in you. They have made up their minds to gather at the Winter Palace. Do not fear anything…accept our humblest petition'. As the crowd of some 120,000 gathered in the hope that the Tsar would accept their demands and possibly even champion their cause, some carried icons and pictures of the Tsar. He was not in the palace and when the marchers refused an order to disperse, the guards opened fire whilst the Cossacks charged amongst them using their swords indiscriminately. With over 100 killed and many more wounded, 'Bloody Sunday' as it came to be called, marked a turning point. Gapon wrote to the Tsar, 'May all the blood which you have spilled fall upon you, you hangman' whilst Nicholas on hearing the news of the slaughter commented, 'My God, how pitiful and sad'.

Afterwards Gapon fled to Geneva in Switzerland where he joined the Socialist Revolutionary Party. However, there were those who thought that he was an agent provocateur secretly in the pay of the Minister of the Interior and an agent of the Okhrana. In 1906, he was assassinated during a visit to Finland.

The consequences

News of the events of Bloody Sunday spread across Russia and workers went on strike and took to the streets to join in demonstrations. Many of the middle classes joined the workers so that by the end of January 1905 more than half a million workers were taking industrial action. Across the country, the district councils, the zemstvas, combined to demand reform whilst in some towns and cities, soviets or workers' councils were set up. In October, a railway strike that started in Moscow developed into a general strike that brought the nation to a standstill. A famous event of the period was the mutiny of the crew of the Russian warship *Potemkin* at the Black Sea port of Odessa. When members of the ship's crew refused to eat rotten biscuits and putrefied meat as ordered by an officer, some of their number were sentenced to death. The firing squad refused to execute their own comrades and instead turned their rifles on their officers. The ship then put to sea and the mutinous crew bombarded coastal towns before seeking asylum in the Rumanian port of Constanza. The Russian film director, Sergei Eisenstein, later turned the episode into an epic film, *The Battleship Potemkin*.

Tsar Nicholas was alarmed by these developments and appointed Sergius Witte to take measures to pacify the people. The moderate Witte advised the Tsar to be conciliatory and grant the Russian people a democratically elected assembly, a Duma, and civil rights in a specially drafted Imperial Manifesto. Meanwhile, the failure of the revolution caused its leaders to escape abroad. Lenin left Russia, travelled in Europe and spent much of his time in Switzerland; after his arrest and exile in Siberia, Trotsky managed to escape and reach Finland; Stalin spent most of these years either in prison or in exile.

The period of failed Dumas

In May 1906, the first Duma met in the Tauride Palace in St Petersburg. The largest party, the Kadets, immediately challenged the Tsar and demanded reform. Nicholas rejected their demands and dissolved the Duma. The promises of the Imperial Manifesto were forgotten when Witte was replaced by the dapper, black-bearded Peter Stolypin who advised the Tsar to return to his old autocratic ways and follow a policy of repression and reform. The second Duma that met for the first time in February 1907 lasted only three months before it too was dissolved. By the time a third Duma assembled in November 1907 the electoral system had been changed so that only the wealthy and landowners retained the right to vote. This meant that the Duma was supportive of the monarchy and did not press for change or reform, which allowed it to survive for five years.

Stolypin was prepared to use terror and intimidation and was determined to suppress the revolutionaries. In some villages, he ordered the flogging of every tenth man as a warning to others and with over 100,000 exiled to the icy wastes of Siberia and some 4,000 executed, it was little wonder that the hangman's noose became nicknamed 'Stolypin's necktie'! In fairness, he did introduce a series of measures intended to remove at least some of the causes of discontent. The education system was reformed, social insurance and sickness benefits introduced and conditions in the army and navy greatly improved. He also encouraged foreign investment in Russian industry and it was during this time that a class of prosperous yeoman farmers first appeared, the kulaks. Even so, his ruthless treatment of revolutionaries and his persecution of the Jews and other non-Russian peoples in the Empire meant that opinion about him was divided. Whilst the nobility thought him too liberal, the majority of Russians resented and feared him. In September 1911, Peter Stolypin was assassinated in the Kiev opera house in the presence of the Tsar. His murder once again left the Tsar vulnerable and he turned increasingly for advice to Gregory Rasputin.

In their different ways, both Witte and Stolypin had served Nicholas well but Rasputin was a very different character. Born in 1872 at Pokrovskoe in western Siberia, he married a peasant girl but then abandoned her and their three children and disappeared. By the time he reappeared, he had become a self-styled mystic and priest who claimed the powers of prophecy and miracle healing. In 1904, Nicholas and Alexandra, who already had four daughters, were blessed with a fifth child, a son. Sadly, the child, Alexis, was cursed with haemophilia, an inherited condition that prevents the blood from clotting. The condition was incurable and this meant that the boy was destined for a life of suffering when even the slightest cut or bruise could lead to a massive loss of blood and a premature death. With doctors powerless to help, the Russian royal family called on Rasputin who seemed able to ease the boy's suffering. Their gratitude was overwhelming and Alexandra urged her husband to accept the priest's advice on matters of state. Unknown to the Tsar and Tsarina, there was another side to the priest's character. Rasputin was a drunkard, a man with the most obscene personal habits, a dirty beard and vile body odour and his life was a round of drunken orgies and loose living. The royal family's association with the priest developed into a national scandal but the Tsarina would not hear a word said against him – to her he was a saintly man who was able to keep her son alive. Abroad, much was made of the scandal, whilst in Russia criticism of Rasputin grew into a major political issue and threatened the very survival of tsarism.

...and what was Stalin up to during this period?

Although Stalin's enthusiasm for Georgian nationalism had waned and been largely replaced by a belief in Marxism, he was far from being considered a prominent member of the Bolshevik hierarchy. He had certainly become a committed Marxist and was prepared to be involved in revolutionary activities. Whilst a student at the seminary in Tbilisi, he had become acquainted with the works of Marks, Engels and other forbidden books and his expulsion was a result of his attempts to spread Marxist propaganda amongst fellow students. As he became increasingly absorbed in politics, so he became obsessed with a hatred of tsarism, the nobility and the middle class who he regarded as the oppressors and exploiters of the working class proletariat. He saw to it too that his image changed from that of a smartly dressed, fresh-faced seminary student to that of a rebel with unkept hair and a dirty tunic with a traditional Marxist red scarf.

In 1900, Stalin was impressed when he first read a copy of Lenin's newspaper, *Iskra*, copies of which were circulated illegally in Russia. His admiration increased further when the two men met at a Marxist conference in 1906. Even so, he was in no sense a leading Bolshevik, as Stalin's propagandists later claimed, but a very ordinary delegate. In a sense, the years prior to the outbreak of war in 1914 were a time of apprenticeship for the embryo revolutionary. It was a period when he busied himself speaking at workers' conferences, agitating and engaging in strike activity and writing an avalanche of articles for the underground press. He was arrested on several occasions and spent time in prison. In 1902, he was arrested by the police for taking part in a demonstration in Batum but he was already in custody when troops opened fire on the crowd, killing 15 and injuring many more. The following year he was sent into exile in the village of Novaya Uda in Siberia. He managed to escape and returned to the Caucasus where local Marxists were involved in acts of open violence. Since money was urgently needed to boost Party funds, Stalin contributed by organizing hold-ups and bank raids and even demanded protection money from the rich. He was also prepared to use blackmail and opened brothels and cashed in on the immoral earnings of prostitutes. Lenin did not approve and in a letter to Stalin said so in the most forceful terms:

> *I am not concerned whether you have affairs with women or not, and I am not concerned whether you change your women as often as you change your shorts. But I am concerned with the good name of the Bolshevik party. I cannot agree that it is the right policy for our party to be concerned with the brothels you have organized!*

Normally Stalin did not accept criticism but he swallowed Lenin's reprimand and ordered his supporters to use more orthodox forms of fund raising.

Stalin first met Trotsky in 1906 and took an instant dislike to the man. It has been claimed that being a poor public speaker himself, he was jealous of Trotsky's cleverness and eloquence. As we shall see, the ill feeling between the two men was to develop into the most bitter of feuds. By now, Stalin had been restored to Lenin's good books and he was asked to edit a new Bolshevik newspaper, *Pravda*. Later, he was to be elected to the policy making group within the party, the Politburo. By 1913, 'My wonderful Georgian', as Lenin called him, could rightly be considered one of the more important Bolsheviks. Arrested again, he was exiled in Turukhansk for four years. Later in 1914, he was transferred to the village of Kureika in the Arctic Circle. During 1916, arrangements were made to draft him into the army but wisely the authorities rejected him for military service and this meant that he was destined to spend the war years in the frozen wastes of distant Siberia.

During 1913, spectacles and great shows of pageantry were arranged to celebrate 300 years of Romanov rule in Russia. Such shows of loyalty were superficial since beneath the surface the Russian people were again in ferment and strikes led to clashes between the police and workers. However, even greater drama was being played out abroad. On 28 June 1914, Archduke Franz Ferdinand, heir to the throne of Austria, was assassinated in Sarajevo, Bosnia. Backed by Germany, it seemed likely that Austria would attack Russia's little ally Serbia. Ominously Rasputin warned, 'Let Papa not plan for war, for with war will come the end of Russia and yourselves...' For once the Tsar did not heed the priest's advice and instead ordered a general mobilization. When Kaiser Wilhelm II of Germany appealed personally to Nicholas to cancel his plans for mobilization, the Tsar refused. On 1 July 1914, Germany declared war on Russia.

Russia and the First World War

The announcement of the outbreak of war was greeted with an upsurge of patriotic fervour as large crowds gathered before the Winter Palace in St Petersburg to sing the national anthem. Because it was German-sounding, Nicholas changed the name of his capital city to Petrograd. With a population of over 150 million, Russia appeared to have inexhaustible manpower but would the so-called 'steamroller army' of 1,400,000 regular and 3,100,000 reservist soldiers fare any better against the Germans than they had against the Japanese ten years earlier? The truth was that Russia was totally unprepared for war. Her army had few good generals, its soldiers were inadequately trained and completely lacking in modern arms and equipment. As supplies of arms and ammunition rapidly dwindled, so it became immediately apparent that Russian industry could not make these losses good. The railway system, with less than half its locomotives serviceable, proved incapable of moving adequate men and munitions to the front. Heavy tax increases and the need for overseas loans imposed a heavy financial burden on the Russian people, whilst inefficiency and corruption did not help the situation.

Before the end of 1914, the Russian armies had twice been heavily defeated at the Battles of Tannenburg and the Masurian Lakes and the disasters continued into 1915 when 4 million of the Tsar's soldiers died on the battlefield. With inadequate food, clothing and weapons and the suffering of the soldiers, the Russian army appeared to be 'drowning in its own blood'. At home, the people turned on those with German-sounding names and burned and looted their homes whilst the German-born Tsarina faced increasing hostility. Determined to show her loyalty to Russia, she worked for war charities and even served as a nurse. News of the disasters at the front did not help and chaos reigned as the price of food and clothing spiralled and black-marketeering became commonplace. As the crisis mounted, Nicholas took a fatal step when he left his wife in Petrograd and personally took command of the exhausted Russian armies. He was no general and his decision failed to increase the will of his hungry and ragged soldiers to resist. Instead their morale gave way and they mutinied and deserted in ever-increasing numbers. In the capital city, even as the country edged closer to revolution, Alexandra continued to give offence by accepting guidance from Rasputin. On 29 December 1916, the debauched priest was assassinated in the most macabre circumstances whilst attending a party given by Felix Yussoupov. Although the assassin, the husband of a niece of the Tsar, first poisoned and then shot his victim at point-blank range, Rasputin still had to be thrown into the freezing waters of the River Neva before he finally died. His death, which left the Tsarina beside herself with grief, was greeted with great rejoicing across the country.

Towards revolution

By the start of 1917, Russia was ripe for revolution and the overthrow of the Tsar appeared to be imminent. The third winter of the war saw the Russian armies in total disarray whilst on the home front, the shortages and suffering of the people grew even more acute. Nicholas could not cope and appeared to be content to sleepwalk aimlessly towards impending disaster. In March 1917, as the Tsar left Petrograd to return to army headquarters, the city erupted with riots, workers took to the streets and the city was soon in the grip of a general strike. Students joined with workers and soldiers to chant 'We want bread!' and 'Down with the Tsar!' In the Duma, the leader of the Social Revolutionary Party, Alexander Kerensky, called for the removal of the Tsar and the formation of a provisional government.

The Julian and Gregorian Calendars

Some books refer to the February Revolution of 1917 since the Russian calendar was then based on the Julian Calendar introduced by Julius Caesar in 46 BC. However, it later became usual to follow the Gregorian Calendar, the new style calendar introduced by Pope Gregory 1582, but this calendar was not used in Russia until 1918. There is a discrepancy of 13 days between the two calendars.

When Nicholas attempted to return to Petrograd, the railway line was blocked by mutinous troops and the imperial train diverted to Pskov. There he was met by generals and representatives of the government who urged him to give up the throne. On 16 March, the Tsar abdicated in favour of his brother, the Grand Duke Michael, but the following day the Grand Duke also wisely renounced the throne. The rule of the Romanov dynasty was finally at an end. Under arrest, Nicholas returned to Petrograd and together with his family was held at Tsarskoe Selo, his country home just outside the city.

News of his abdication was greeted with great enthusiasm across Russia. At the front, discipline broke down as thousands of soldiers deserted and made their way home. In Moscow and other towns and cities, the workers formed soviets whilst in the countryside the peasants seized land. In an uncertain situation, the people looked to Kerensky and his provisional government for leadership.

From the start, relations between the new provisional government and the Petrograd Soviet were strained. Prince Lvov, appointed to head a provisional government of moderate socialists, was in a difficult situation since the Soviet was dominated by the left – Social Revolutionaries, Mensheviks and a generous sprinkling of firebrand Bolsheviks. The government set out its programme of reform that included an amnesty for all political prisoners, freedom of speech and the right to form trades union. It also indicated its intention to hold elections for a Constitutional Assembly based on universal suffrage and a secret vote. However, by deciding to continue the war against Germany, the government committed a major folly that was soon to lead to his own demise.

During this time, the Bolshevik leaders had been making their way back to Russia from their places of exile. These included Vladimir Ilyich Ulyanov, who had taken the name Lenin, and Leon Davidovich Bronstein, better known as Trotsky. Lenin, whose brother had been executed for his part in a plot to assassinate the Tsar, came from a middle-class background and was a qualified lawyer; Trotsky, a fiery orator, was a Ukrainian from a Jewish peasant family. Lenin, the Bolshevik leader, arrived in Petrograd to a tumultuous reception on 16 April 1917. During the weeks that followed, he first published his April Thesis that demanded the transfer of power from the provisional government to the soviets, since this would give him the means to influence and organize the workers. To win support, Lenin also made use of popular slogans, 'Peace, bread and land' and 'All power to the soviets'. July was a month of strikes and demonstrations and it was during this time that the Russian army suffered a further series of heavy defeats. At this point Prince Lvov resigned and was replaced as prime minister by Alexander Kerensky. Amongst those who thought Kerensky too weak to deal with the Bolsheviks was General Lavr Kornilov. Described as 'a man with a lion's heart and the brains of a sheep', together with other generals and industrialists he made plans to march on Petrograd and overthrow Kerensky's government. As a crisis threatened, groups of workers formed units known as Red Guards to oppose Kornilov's attempted coup. In fact, there was no fighting and whilst the episode came to nothing, it placed the Bolsheviks in a far stronger position than before. From his hiding place Lenin wrote: 'History will not forgive us if we don't seize power now'.

THE OCTOBER REVOLUTION

In October, Lenin returned to Petrograd and began to plan his revolution. A Military Revolutionary Committee set up under Trotsky was housed in the Smolny Institute, formerly a convent school for the daughters of the wealthy. The Committee set the date for a Bolshevik uprising for the night of 6/7 November and its start was to be signalled by a salvo from the guns of the cruiser Aurora. Whilst these preparations were taking place, elsewhere in Russia life went on as usual. Although everyone seemed to realize that a revolution was imminent, Kerensky did nothing. On the evening of 6 November, Bolshevik Red Guards moved into all the strategic points in Petrograd and by the morning the railway stations, banks, power stations and telephone exchanges had been seized. During this time the guns of the Aurora were trained on the Winter Palace, where the members of the provisional government had gathered. At 9 p.m., the ship fired its guns and the Red Guards easily occupied the building. Kerensky made his escape in a car borrowed from the American embassy and now, late in the day, tried to muster support. The Bolshevik revolution had been accomplished by relatively few men and with the minimum of bloodshed. Within a very short time, life in Petrograd returned to normal whilst elsewhere in Russia people were either unsure or unaware of what had happened. In reality, the revolutionaries had gained only limited success and were far from being in control of the country. Lenin and his Bolsheviks still had a long, hard and bitter road to travel.

Stalin's role in these events

In March 1917, when news reached Stalin of the abdication of the Tsar, he escaped from his place of imprisonment and headed for Petrograd. There he found that apart from himself, Lev Kamenev was the only other leading Bolshevik in the city. Together they decided to encourage the Bolsheviks to support Kerensky and urged the Russian soldiers to continue in the war against Germany. Lenin, who had plans to remove Kerensky and bring about his own Bolshevik revolution, was dumbfounded by their decisions and criticized both men for their errors. It is said that after Lenin's reprimand Stalin 'slunk away like a kicked dog' and little more was heard of him until after the upheavals of October 1917.

3

Civil war – the death of Lenin and the power struggle

This chapter will cover:
- *the fate of the Constituent Assembly*
- *Lenin's plans for post-revolutionary Russia*
- *Brest-Litovsk – the peace treaty with Germany*
- *the coming of civil war*
- *the murder of the Romanov family*
- *Lenin's death and the power struggle that followed.*

> *...I suggest that comrades think about a way of removing Stalin...and appointing another man who differs from Comrade Stalin in being more tolerant, more loyal, more polite and more considerate of his comrades...*
>
> From Lenin's *Political Testament*

The situation at the end of 1917

Although it was to result ultimately in the establishment of the first Communist state and have worldwide repercussions, at the time the Bolshevik revolution of October 1917 might have been considered a non-event. Its success was achieved with far greater ease than expected and hardly any bloodshed. Throughout Russia, the daily life of the people appeared to continue much as before but for many it was a time of uncertainty and concern for the future. Even though Kerensky had failed to muster enough support to prevent Lenin's take over, across the country several groups were gathering strength to challenge the Bolsheviks and crush the revolution. Although the Bolsheviks had gained control of Petrograd, revolutionary fervour had only just started to spread to other towns and cities whilst in rural areas, the peasants largely continued to support the Social Revolutionaries. It should be remembered that a large area of western Russia was under German control and many of the non-Russian peoples of Finland and the Ukraine saw the upheaval as an opportunity to demand independence.

In an unreal situation, Lenin began to issue scores of decrees and directives that he could in no way enforce. Trotsky called it 'revolution by telegraph'. Some Bolsheviks thought that the only way out of the chaos was to form a coalition with other left-wing parties but Lenin would have none of this. He argued that in such a period of uncertainty, the Bolsheviks could only bring about a dictatorship of the proletariat if they vigorously enforced their decisions and crushed their opponents. Lenin had earlier promised elections to a Constituent Assembly so that the framework of a new constitution could be drawn up.

The short-lived Constituent Assembly

The elections of November 1917 were, until very recent times, the first and only truly democratic elections ever held in Russia. At the polls, the Social Revolutionaries won a resounding victory with 370 seats. The Bolsheviks gained only 175 whilst the Kadets, Mensheviks and other small parties shared the remaining 162 seats between them. For his party to win less than a quarter of the 707 seats came as a stunning blow to Lenin but he was far from finished. The first meeting of the Constituent Assembly took place on 5 January 1918. Within the building there was chaos as Bolshevik deputies continually disrupted proceedings whilst in the corridors deputies had to run a gauntlet of drunk and abusive Red Guards. On the following day, Bolshevik soldiers barred the entrance and the Assembly was dissolved. Afterwards Lenin declared, 'Only scoundrels and imbeciles can think that the proletariat must first win a majority of votes in elections under the bourgeois yoke...and only then seek power'.

The Bolshevik leader next turned his attention to the need to change Russia into a Communist society. An eight-hour day was introduced as well as a system of social insurance intended to cover old age, sickness and injury, unemployment and the needs of widows and orphans. All titles and class distinctions were ended and 'comrade' became the usual style of address. In the armed services, all ranks were abolished together with decorations and the need to salute officers. Banks and railways were nationalized and in rural areas all landowners' estates were confiscated without compensation and the land shared amongst the peasants. In urban areas workers occupied the factories and workshops. The Russian Orthodox Church did not escape Lenin's attention. Church schools were taken over by the State, Church lands were confiscated and marriage became a civil and not a religious ceremony.

Lenin was well aware that some might be planning to overthrow his new Bolshevik regime. In December 1917, the Commission Against Counter-Revolution, Sabotage and Speculation was established under the leadership of Felix Dzerzhinsky, the son of a rich Lithuanian landowner. Better known as the Cheka, it employed some 30,000 agents to root out and remove the enemies of the revolution. Its headquarters were situated in the offices of a former insurance company in Lubyanka Street and this was soon to become the most notorious address in Moscow. In July 1918, Lenin finally gave Russia a new constitution when it became the Russian Soviet Federal Socialist Republic or RSFSR. At the same time all other political parties were banned and the country became a Communist controlled one-party state. However, it should be remembered that although fighting along the Eastern Front had ceased, strictly speaking Russia was still at war with Germany and to ensure the continued success of the revolution, Lenin needed to negotiate a peace treaty with Germany.

The Treaty of Brest-Litovsk, 1918

Once the Germans had indicated their willingness to open negotiations, arrangements were made for delegates to meet at Brest-Litovsk (present-day Brest in Balarus). Trotsky, who had been advised to accept any conditions demanded by Germany no matter how severe, led the Russian delegation. In fact the terms demanded were so harsh that one Russian delegate committed suicide and Trotsky pressed for a continuation of the war. The disagreement amongst Bolshevik leaders led to a delay and so the Germans

Figure 3.1 The territory lost by Russia as a result of the Treaty of Brest-Litovsk.

resumed their advance and threatened to demand even tougher terms. In the end, Lenin insisted on the acceptance of the terms and the treaty was finally signed on 3 March 1918. The Bolshevik leader refused to read it, saying, 'I shall neither read it nor carry out its terms whenever there is a chance not to do so'.

By the treaty, Russia surrendered Poland, the Baltic provinces of Estonia, Latvia and Lithuania, Finland and parts of the Caucasus. A promise was also made to recognize the independence of the Ukraine. Altogether Russia lost a quarter of all her territory in Europe, a third of her population, over half her industry and four-fifths of her coal mines. In addition, Germany demanded the payment of 6,000 billion gold marks by way of reparations.

To the wartime Allies – Britain, France and the United States – the withdrawal of Russia at such a critical stage of the war came as a bitter blow since it meant that German armies could now be released for use on the Western Front. In a strange way, Germany too became a loser since the end of the war meant that thousands of German prisoners-of-war were released. Many of these prisoners had witnessed the Russian revolution at first hand and returned home with new and dangerous ideas. Once back in Germany some were not keen to return to their units and began to cause unrest.

The civil war

The elections to the Constituent Assembly in 1917 had shown that across Russia as a whole, the Bolsheviks were an unpopular minority and by wrecking the Assembly they had indicated their willingness to ignore and override the wishes of the Russian people. Lenin was very aware that he faced the prospect of a counter-revolution. As anti-Bolshevik forces began to mobilize, it became evident that the Social Revolutionaries, Mensheviks, Kadets, the renegade generals of the former tsarist armies and those who remained loyal to the Tsar were hopelessly divided and there was no way of bringing together their varied interests. By the end of 1918, several groups, collectively known as Whites, had begun to campaign independently against the Bolshevik Red Army. The Allies, who had neither forgotten nor forgiven the betrayal of Brest-Litovsk, sent units to fight in Russia and so hopefully ensure a White victory. In addition, the Bolsheviks had infuriated Britain and France by confiscating Allied-owned

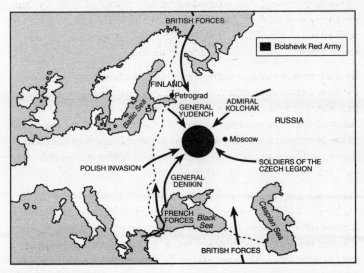

Figure 3.2 The civil war, 1918–21.

property and refusing to repay loans previously made to the tsarist government. Abroad, there was concern about the safety of Tsar Nicholas and his family and alarm at rumours about the behaviour of the dreaded Cheka.

In the south, General Anton Denekin, aided by British and French troops as well as Cossacks, tried to set up a military dictatorship whilst to the north a White army under General Nikolai Yudenich advanced to attack Petrograd. In the east, Admiral Aleksandr Kolchak set up a government in Omsk and gained some early victories over the Red Army. He was helped by the Czech Legion that consisted of some 40,000 Czech prisoners-of-war and deserters from the Austrian army being held in Russia. On their release, they were anxious to get home but, delayed by the Bolsheviks, they mutinied and joined Kolchak's forces.

Lenin realized that he needed to recruit a well-trained army and ensure that it was adequately supplied with weapons and food. The task of organizing the Red Army was delegated to Trotsky, who saw to it that men were conscripted or forced to serve in the army by the Cheka. To cope with a shortage of officers, he enlisted many of those who had earlier served in the old tsarist army whilst he himself directed military operations from an armoured train that toured the battle areas. In order to overcome shortages, Lenin introduced a range of severe economic measures that he called War Communism. As factories were geared to war production, so workers were forced to work excessive hours without wages. Their reward was a ration of food, clothing and lodgings. Those too old or otherwise unable to work could only survive by selling their remaining possessions. In the countryside, soldiers were authorized to confiscate crops and livestock and often failed to leave sufficient for the peasants' own needs or even seed for future crops. The reaction of the peasants to these unpopular measures was to grow fewer crops and hide what they had. This meant that food shortages became even worse.

'The Red Terror'

An attempt on Lenin's life, together with the assassination of Moisei Uritsky, head of the Petrograd Cheka, gave rise to concern and as the unrest increased further, so the Bolshevik leader was forced to resort to terror. The main instruments of terror were the Red Army and Dzerzhinsky's Cheka and the head of the secret police showed no compassion as he dealt with those considered to be enemies of the revolution. He issued a directive, 'Do not concern yourselves with forms of revolutionary justice. We have no need for justice now... I propose, I demand the use of the revolutionary sword that will put an end to all counter-revolutionaries'. The independence of trade unions was brought to an end and those who protested or went on strike were treated as traitors and shot without trial. A proof of guilt was not required and people were executed because they appeared to belong to the wrong class or possess some wealth.

Across Russia, the bourgeoisie were driven from their homes, deprived of food and forced to undertake degrading work. Although the activities of the Cheka led to protests from some Bolsheviks, no steps were taken to curb their activities and during this period an estimated 7,000 people were shot or simply disappeared. Amongst the victims of the Red Terror was the Russian royal family.

The end of the Romanovs

During the summer of 1918, units of the Czech Legion moved towards Ekaterinburg where Tsar Nicholas and his family were being held. Shamefully treated, they had hoped to be allowed to leave for Britain but King George V refused to provide them with asylum. As the Czechs approached, the local Bolsheviks panicked since they realized that the rescue of the royal family would prove a rallying point for the Whites. On the night of 16 July 1918, the royal family – the Tsar, Tsarina and their children Olga, Tatiana, Maria, Anastasia and Alexis – were ordered into the cellar where they were murdered. Those who survived the first volley of bullets were finished off with bayonets and rifle butts before their bodies were thrown into a disused mine shaft. Eight days later, Ekaterinburg fell to the Whites. Afterwards rumours persisted that one of the Tsar's daughters had survived the slaughter and two years later a girl claiming to be Anastasia appeared in Berlin. Named Anna Anderson, the girl persisted with her claim until her death in 1989.

A great deal of controversy surrounds the fate of the imperial family but in 1991 their remains were discovered and confirmed by DNA testing. They were reinterred in St Catherine's Chapel in St Petersburg.

Six weeks after the murder of the Tsar and his family an attempt was made on the life of Lenin. After speaking at a labour rally in Moscow, he was shot and seriously wounded by Fanya Kaplan. The assassin came from an odd background. Born into a poor peasant family, her parents left her behind when they emigrated to the United States. Afterwards she became involved in politics and in 1906 was arrested for her part in a plot to assassinate the Tsar. She was sentenced to life imprisonment in Siberia with hard labour. Released at the time of the March Revolution, she was infuriated by Lenin's decision to close down the Constitutional Assembly and considered him to be 'a traitor to the revolution'. After interrogation by the Cheka, she was executed.

Meanwhile, as the civil war dragged on so the Red Army gradually won the upper hand. Denikin was unpopular with the Russian people and as his forces disintegrated, the remnants fled across the Black Sea to find refuge in Turkey whilst their leader sought asylum abroad. He died in 1947. Yudenich's attempt to take Petrograd also petered out and as his forces retreated into Estonia, he fled to France where he died in 1933. Kolchak, who fared the worst, lost his early gains, fell into the hands of the Red Army and was shot by firing squad in 1920. With all hopes of a White victory gone, British and French forces were finally withdrawn and the civil war final came to an end in 1922 when the Red Army entered Vladivostok.

The reasons for the success of the Red Army are plain to see. Apart from a hatred of Bolshevism, the Whites had no common purpose, were disunited and often showed a lack of determination. Their conflicting interests meant that their armies fought as uncoordinated units and they had no military commander of the calibre of Trotsky. In the long run, the intervention of foreign troops on behalf of the Whites was to their disadvantage since it made the Reds appear more patriotic and independent. Much credit must also go to Trotsky's leadership of the Red Army, and severe as it was, to Lenin's War Communism that succeeded in providing for the needs of the army at the most critical time. The Reds also had the advantage of controlling the railway system that made it possible to transfer soldiers from one front to another and ensure that their fighting men were adequately supplied. During the civil war, both sides committed acts of brutality and there were countless atrocities. Neither side tolerated neutrality and those who were not for were considered against and shot out of hand. For the peasants there was little to choose between the savagery of the Whites and the severity of the Reds who had requisitioned their crops. Both sides conscripted those unwilling to fight and it was generally a choice of enlistment or execution.

By the end of the civil war, Russia was in a state of total exhaustion and the economy was close to total collapse. Industry was at a near standstill as it began the process of converting back to a peacetime economy whilst the peasants saw no point in producing crops other than for their own needs. In the urban centres, workers risked being stricken by epidemics and the scourge of typhus was ever present. Famine led to hunger and starvation and tens of thousands of people died of malnutrition. As some reached the depths of despair and the limits of their endurance, they resorted to cannibalism and traded in human flesh. Across the country there was unrest and even acts of defiance against the Communist regime and in particular the excesses of War Communism. At the Communist Party Conference in 1921, Lenin notes that, 'The poverty of the working class was never so vast and acute...' and in March of that year the anger of the people finally exploded at Kronstadt.

The Kronstadt rising, 1921

The sailors and workers at Kronstadt, a fortress town and naval base on Kotlin Island in the Gulf of Finland, had originally been amongst the staunchest supporters of the revolution. However, by March 1922 the savagery of the civil war, the ruthless application of War Communism and the apparent stranglehold of the Communist Party on Russian domestic affairs had brought disenchantment. Using slogans such as 'Soviets without Communists', they demonstrated openly against Lenin's regime and made a list of demands that included free elections, and freedom of speech and of the press. Mikhail Kalinin, a senior Party official, was sent to warn the people of Kronstadt about their behaviour and hopefully prevent any further embarrassment. His words had little effect and consequently Trotsky sent them a threatening ultimatum. Two days later, the Red Army launched an assault on the garrison. Between December and March the sea is frozen over and this meant that the Bolshevik soldiers were able to move across the ice. For the next ten days there followed hand-to-hand street fighting before the rebels were overcome. The

Communists immediately took their revenge and the ringleaders, together with many others, were arrested and shot. Publicly Lenin claimed that the Kronstadt uprising was a bourgeois-inspired plot but privately he recognized that it was a warning and described it as 'the flash that lit up reality better than anything else'. It was time to compromise and almost immediately he introduced a New Economic Policy that was a turnabout and in part a return to capitalist ways.

Lenin's New Economic Policy

In order to encourage the peasants to grow more food, Lenin agreed that they could sell their surplus crops on the open market and consequently supplies of food began to increase. Small factories were returned to private ownership and a system of bonus incentives introduced. Once again private trade was encouraged so that shops and markets began to flourish and in order to convince the Russian people of the stability of their currency, the rouble was revalued. If Lenin was allowing a modest return to capitalism, it was only on the fringes of the economy since the State retained control over the 'commanding heights' – transport, big business and heavy industry. Whilst the New Economic Policy brought some respite to the hard-pressed people, it was really the generosity of other nations that relieved the suffering caused by famine. The United States, Britain, France and Italy all sent large quantities of food, clothing and medicines. The American Relief Administration alone provided millions of dollars worth of aid whilst using the offices of the International Red Cross, the Norwegian explorer and philanthropist, Fridtjof Nansen, organized relief work and supplied some 80,000 tonnes of food. At one time over 10 million Russians were dependent on overseas aid.

In 1923, the Russian constitution was revised so that the country became a federation of seven republics, the Union of Soviet Socialist Republics, the USSR. Each republic was to be ruled by its own Soviet representing the workers and peasants and would send delegates to the All-Union Congress of Soviets in the country's new capital city, Moscow. In reality, Russia was now governed by the Communist Party and the most influential men were those who belonged to the policy making Politburo. The Cheka was replaced by the Organization for State Political Administration, the OGPU, but the change in name did not change its purpose or its methods.

After the attempt on his life in 1918, Lenin's health gradually deteriorated and in May 1922 he suffered the first of several strokes. During this period, his devoted wife Nadya Krupskaya, who was always at his side, nursed him. Although only able to speak with difficulty and walk a few steps at a time, he insisted on working at his office in the Kremlin. On 21 January 1924, at the age of 53, Lenin died. His passing was mourned across Russia and over a million people attended his funeral procession. His body was embalmed and placed in a mausoleum in Moscow's Red Square where it was to become a place of pilgrimage. Petrograd, the birthplace of the revolution, was renamed Leningrad in his honour. Lenin's great achievement was the creation of the first socialist state, the Soviet Union, ruled according to his interpretation of the theories of Karl Marx, now called Marx-Leninism. For a time after his death his policies continued to be followed and Russian living standards marginally improved. Winston Churchill, an outspoken opponent of Bolshevism, observed, 'The Russian people were left floundering in a bog. Their worst misfortune was his birth...their next worse, his death'. Others have been less harsh in their assessment of Lenin. Victor Serge, a friend and fellow revolutionary, said of Lenin's skills as a public speaker:

He was neither a great orator nor a first class lecturer. He employed no rhetoric and did not try to rouse his audience. His vocabulary was that of a newspaper article and he was inclined to be repetitive... He was a man of basic simplicity, talking to you people honestly and with the sole purpose of convincing you.

The historian Geoffrey Hosking wrote:

Lenin shared with previous Russian revolutionaries the belief in a humane and democratic future society. Where he differed from them was in a hard-headed realism and the determination to achieve power at all costs.

And Stalin's view of Lenin:

...by creating a Republic of Soviets he gave a practical demonstration to the oppressed masses of the world that the hope of deliverance is not lost... He thus fired the hearts of workers and peasants of the whole world with the hope of liberation.

The power struggle – Trotsky versus Stalin

The death of Lenin in January 1924 threw the Communist leadership into confusion. During the final months of his life and as his condition worsened, members of the Politburo had been plotting and scheming as they jockeyed for position in the leadership struggle that was to come. Many Russians saw it as a one-horse race with Trotsky as the only heir apparent and Lenin's obvious successor. Identified by his pince-nez spectacles, peaked cap and goatee beard, he had latterly been a close associate of Lenin and was popular with the military because of his successful leadership of the Red Army during the civil war. Then there were those who remembered that prior to 1917 he had been a Menshevik and had often openly and bitterly disagreed with Lenin. Others in the frame included Lev Kamenev and Grigori Zinoviev who had both opposed Lenin's plan to seize power in October 1917 because they thought the move premature, and Nikolai Bukharin, the Communist Party theorist and editor of Pravda. Two outsiders were Andrei Rykov and Grigori Pyayakov who were in their twenties and seen by some as the rising stars of the Party. Few noticed that behind the scenes Stalin had manoeuvered himself into a most advantageous position. Although he had played little part in the events of October 1917, because he was a Georgian and Russian was his second language he seemed ideal for appointment as Commissar of Nationalities with the responsibility for non-Russian peoples. Two years later he joined the Politburo and in 1922, he became the General Secretary of the Communist Party, a position that gave him control of the Party machine and considerable power to influence appointments, recommend promotions and, when necessary, arrange dismissals. He used his position to place friends in important positions in local and central government, fully expecting that when the time came his patronage would be repaid. Apart from feathering his own nest, during the last months of Lenin's life he had always remained close at hand and virtually became his leader's gaoler. He kept a close eye on all communications received and sent by his leader, bullied those around Lenin's bedside and was excessively rude to his wife, Krupskaya. The sickly Lenin was infuriated by his behaviour and belatedly recognized what was going on behind his back and the danger of Stalin's blatant scheming. From his sickbed, Lenin dictated a letter to the Politburo that he wanted to be read to delegates at the pending Twelfth Party Congress. The letter came to be regarded as his political testament.

In order to lessen the chances of conflict or small sections acquiring excessive importance, Lenin first suggested a broadening of the membership of the Central Committee. He next provided his own assessment of the qualities of the members of the Politburo. He wrote:

> *Comrade Stalin, having become General-Secretary, has unlimited authority concentrated in his hands and I am not sure whether he will always be capable of using that authority with sufficient caution. Comrade Trotsky, on the other hand, is distinguished not only by an outstanding personality. He is personally perhaps the most capable man in the present Central Committee but he has displayed excessive self-assurance with the purely administrative side of the work. These two qualities of the two outstanding leaders of the present Central Committee can inadvertently lead to a split, and if our Party does not take steps to prevent this, the split may come unexpectedly.*

A week later after Stalin had again been abusive to Krupskaya, Lenin added a postscript to his letter:

> *Stalin is too rude and this defect...becomes quite intolerable in a General-Secretary. That is why I suggest that comrades think about a way of removing Stalin from the post and appointing another man who differs from Comrade Stalin in being more tolerant, more loyal, more polite and more considerate of his comrades...From the standpoint of safeguards against a split between Stalin and Trotsky, it is not a minor detail that can become extremely important.*

Stalin must have winced as he heard the contents of Lenin's letter read from the rostrum. Indeed, it might have spelled the end of his political career had not Zinoviev stood to defend Stalin's behaviour and express the view that Lenin's fears were unfounded. As it was, Stalin said that he would mend his ways and was allowed to remain as General-Secretary of the Party. In spite of the advantages gained from his position, Stalin still had good cause to be concerned about his rival. Strangely Trotsky, who was not without loyal supporters and could depend on the backing of the military, showed little enthusiasm for the fight that lay ahead.

For a while there followed an uneasy peace. Against the wishes of Krupskaya, Stalin turned Lenin's funeral into a staged ceremony in which he played the central role. In his funeral oration, he said, 'Comrade Lenin ordained to us the unity of our Party...We vow to you, Comrade Lenin, that we shall fulfil honourably your commandment...'. Yet even as he spoke, behind the scenes there was already much scheming, double dealing and acts of treachery and betrayal taking place.

There were a number of issues that divided the Party. In the first place, Trotsky wanted to see a broad-based government working towards achieving the wishes of the workers; Stalin favoured government by a centralized bureaucracy since clearly this would give him the greatest influence. Trotsky wanted to use the Bolshevik revolution in Russia as a springboard to bring about similar revolutions elsewhere in Europe; Stalin's view was that it was first necessary to successfully establish socialism in the Soviet Union or, as he called it, 'Socialism in one country'. Within the Politburo there were differences of opinion about the future direction of the Russian economy. Stalin was convinced that hostile capitalist countries intent on overthrowing the Communist regime surrounded Russia and he considered it essential that his country pressed ahead with the rapid industrialization since this would provide the military might needed to protect it from foreign enemies. To achieve this, he recognized that it might be necessary to introduce measures to force the peasants, who were still enjoying the advantages of the New Economic Policy, to produce sufficient food for the industrial workers in the towns and cities.

During the period immediately after Lenin's death, the Soviet Union was first governed jointly by a triumvirate of Kamenev, Zinoviev and Stalin, whose common aim was to oppose Trotsky. Slowly but surely they outmanoeuvred Trotsky and in 1925, he was forced to resign as Commissar for Military and Naval Affairs and was made responsible for a national programme of electrification that was relatively unimportant. He took his demotion without protest. During 1926, the struggle for the leadership intensified as Kamenev, Zinoviev and Trotsky joined forces against Stalin. Stalin won the contest hands down and saw to it that his opponents were dismissed from the Politburo and even expelled from the Party. Finally, in 1929, Trotsky was banished from the Soviet Union and after spending some time in Turkey and France finally settled in Mexico. From his place of exile, he continued to pour scorn on Stalin. Showing humility, Kamenev and Zinoviev begged for and received Stalin's forgiveness whilst Bukharin remained his close ally. One by one the unprincipled schemer dismissed and replaced them with men on whose unquestioning support he could depend – men such as Mikhail Kalinin, Vyacheslav Molotov and Kliment Voroshilov. All along, Stalin's opponents had underestimated him and their hatred of Trotsky had blinded them to the ambitions of Stalin. Now it was all too late and Stalin was supreme in Russia. In effect, he was already a dictator.

The Russian people who had lived through war, revolution and civil war now hoped for a period of respite under the leadership of a man who would improve their conditions. To them, Stalin seemed a moderate man who would bring much needed stability to their homeland.

4

Stalin's economic policies (1) – the collectivization of agriculture

This chapter will cover:
- *the process and system of collectivization*
- *the fate of the kulaks*
- *the extent of the success of collectivization*
- *the impact of collectivization on the Russian people.*

> *...I heard a (kulak) woman shouting with an unearthly voice. The woman... held a flaming sheaf of grain in her hands... She tossed the burning sheaf on to the thatched roof of the house. 'Infidels! Murderers! We have worked all our lives for our house, You won't have it. The flames will have it!*
>
> From *I Chose Freedom* by V. Kravchenko, a high-placed Communist official who defected to the United States in the late 1940s

Introduction

As we have seen, Stalin supported the policy of 'Socialism in One Country' and his aim was to convert the Soviet Union into a modern industrial state. With his country surrounded by hostile capitalist states, he felt that there was no time to lose and he told his people, 'We are fifty to a hundred years behind the advanced countries. We must make good this difference in ten years. Either we do it or we shall be crushed.' His intention was first to erase all traces of capitalism and then, without regard to cost or human suffering, bring about 'a revolution from above' based on centralized planning controlled by the government. In order to bring about the industrialization of the Soviet Union, it would first be necessary to take steps to ensure that the workers in factories and other plants would be adequately fed and to achieve this a programme of major agricultural reform would be necessary.

Russia was largely an agricultural country and after the October Revolution, the land of the former great landowners was shared amongst the peasants. This meant that each unit was small, usually little more than a smallholding on which each peasant family grew enough for itself with a little left over to buy essential extras such as salt, cloth and other household requirements. Room for improvement was limited since the peasants had little knowledge of modern farming methods and possessed little or no machinery. The system was primitive and inefficient and since it was made up of small units, there was little chance it would ever be run efficiently and produce sufficient food to feed the workers in the expanding industrial areas. Have no doubt, the peasants were quite content with the situation that existed, particularly after Lenin's introduction of his New Economic Policy that allowed them to sell their surplus crops on the open market. Many became well off and some members of the kulak class extremely rich. The kulaks, who had long existed in Russia, were peasants who had worked hard, done well for themselves and become wealthy. Other poor peasants were offended by the prosperity of the kulaks, were envious of them and considered them greedy.

After the revolution, agriculture began to recover far more quickly than industry and this led to an imbalance. As the peasants produced more crops so the price of food fell but since factory-made goods remained scarce, their price continued to rise. Trotsky illustrated what might eventually happen using the analogy of a pair of scissors with one blade representing the price of food and the other, the price of manufactured goods. He argued that as the blades opened so the income of the price of food would fall and the peasants would be unwilling to produce extra food. Further, if the blades opened too far then there would be trouble between the industrial workers and the peasants. To counter this, in 1924 the Soviet government took steps to reduce the price of manufactured goods and this produced a temporary solution but the problem still remained. Stalin's remedy was to 'guide peasant farming towards socialism'. The revolution had endowed the peasants with land, now Stalin was about to take it back. Vyacheslav Molotov was given overall responsibility for the steps to be taken and it was a task to which he applied himself with diligence and relentless ferocity!

Collectivization – the theory

Put very simply, collectivization was an attempt to improve agricultural productivity by bringing together smallholdings to form larger farms. It had long been a principle of Marxism and whilst Lenin sought to win over the peasants by argument and use voluntary means, Stalin wanted to press ahead irrespective of their willingness even though this would mean enforcing a new farming system on 100 million peasants and the elimination of a social class. Although he hoped that peasants would form collective farms voluntarily, Stalin realized that the implementation of his plans would mean war since if the peasants resisted, they would be forced to surrender their land in order to create vast collective farms or *kolkhozee*. *Kolkhozee* is the plural of *kolkhoz* and an abbreviation of *kollektivnoe khozyaistwo*, a collective farm. By using much larger units and through the pooling of land and livestock, Stalin sought to take advantages of the economies of scale and, as a result, agriculture would become more efficient and increase output. In their new situation, peasants would become wage-labourers and their earnings would depend on the profitability of the *kolkhoz*. Living in village-type communities, any profit made would be reinvested so that eventually the communities would possess nurseries, schools, clinics and hospitals. The *kolkhozee* would also be permitted to use machinery provided by Mechanical and Tractor Stations, MTS, that would be established across the country. In addition to *kolkhozee*, it was also intended to set up *sovkhoze*. These state farms would employ workers rather than peasants and pay them a fixed wage. The majority of peasants were unhappy with the idea of surrendering their land and animals but, as we shall see, the greatest opposition came from the kulaks. This was understandable since they had most to lose!

Collectivization – the practice

It was not until December 1929 and just a few days after Stalin's fiftieth birthday that the Party's Central Committee ordered the start of enforced collectivization. Party officials went into the countryside and, backed up by the OGPU and Red Army units, began to ruthlessly enforce the collectivization of all farming land and the confiscation of grain and livestock. The reaction of many peasants and the kulaks in particular was to sell their grain off cheaply, slaughter their animals and destroy what few implements they possessed. An enraged Stalin told the Party, 'We now have the opportunity to mount a decisive offensive against the kulaks, to break their resistance and destroy them as a class'. In January 1930 he approved the resolution On Measures for the Elimination of Kulak Households in Districts of Comprehensive Collectivization. The kulaks were about to be hit by a 'red holocaust'.

A Bolshevik poster entitled 'Kulak blood-sucker' shows a bloated peasant sitting on sacks of grain.

Making no concessions and showing no mercy, OGPU agents and Communist Party activists moved into the countryside to drive kulak families from their homes. They were not to be harassed or forced into collectives, they were to be exterminated or, as Alexander Solzenitsyn later wrote, 'All had to go down the same road, to the same common destruction.' Kulaks who resisted were deemed counter-revolutionaries and shot out of hand whilst their families were sent to the remotest regions of the country. The remainder, whole families and even pregnant women and women with babies in arms, were herded into cattle trucks and deported to Siberia. In sub-zero temperatures, thousands, particularly the very young and very old, perished on the journey and those that survived were placed in Corrective Labour Camps run by the OGPU. Known by the acronym GULAGS, their unfortunate inmates were used as slave labour and supervised by ruthless camp guards who referred to their prisoners as 'white coal'. Even more unfortunate were those dumped in desolate, uninhabited tundra regions and abandoned there to survive as best they could. With no existing human habitation, they were at the mercy of guards and their dogs. In temperatures as low as – 40 degrees centigrade, thousands died of exposure and starvation and those who survived did so by living in holes and trying to grow food by digging into the ground with their own bare hands. The unfortunate kulaks fell victims not only to the OGPU and Party officials but also to malicious village peasants who had been jealous of their wealth. Some of these kept watch and delighted in detaining kulaks attempting to escape. Some well-off peasants handed over their land and livestock and pleaded with those in charge not to consider them kulaks. There are numerous accounts of the atrocities that occurred:

> *...the family was lined up outside their farmhouse by Stalin's men. The father and mother were shot immediately in full view of their children, thus being punished for the crime of successfully farming 200 acres of land.*

> *Stalin: Man of Steel* by Elizabeth Mauchline Roberts, 1968

> *So one family was deported because it owned a cow and a calf; another because its mare had a foal; another because a woman helped a family with the harvest. A peasant with eight acres was forced to clear the railway line of snow. On his return, he found all his property seized...*

> *Famine in Russia* by Brian Moynahan, 1975

> *All over the country, as women howled and sobbed, the*
> *unfortunates were loaded onto carts, which moved out of the village*
> *under the watchful eyes of the OGPU. People gazed round the*
> *empty houses that had been their family homes for centuries. They*
> *were leaving behind a life that they would never see again.*
>
>

Stalin by Edvard Radzinsky, 1996

How many kulaks died remains uncertain with estimates ranging from 5 million to twice that number. The irony was that in eliminating that class, Stalin had deprived his country of its most skilled and productive farmers! Next the Communist dictator turned on the other peasants who became compulsorily forced into collectives and were about to experience a second period of serfdom. Although there were those who entered into the idea of collectivization with enthusiasm, they were many who were not prepared to over-exert themselves in the interests of the Communist state. As a result, seeds went unsown, crops were left unharvested and livestock left untended as the peasants left vast areas untended and refused to work and grow crops. To make matters worse, the quotas of grain demanded from each collective were unrealistic and had no chance of being filled and this led to OGPU and Communist officials visiting rural areas and confiscating all the food they could find. Anyone caught hoarding food was liable to be sent to prison or even shot. Stalin was determined to force the peasantry into submission even if this meant starving them to death. The result was famine across the country as people struggled to survive by eating vegetation, their pets and sometimes even their own dead!

For a time, Stalin was forced to relent in his ruthless drive towards collectivization and once again allowed peasants to cultivate their own small plots of land, grow crops and keep cattle. However, this should not be regarded as a part return to a watered-down version of Lenin's New Economic Policy, far from it. He blamed the excesses on over-enthusiastic Party officials and, in 1930, wrote in *Pravda*:

> *The fact that by February of this year 50 per cent of the peasant*
> *farms have been collectivized is a tremendous achievement... Such*
> *success sometimes led to a spirit of vanity and conceit: We can do*
> *anything! There's nothing we can't do. People became intoxicated*
> *by such successes; they became dizzy with success, lose all sense of*
> *proportion and the ability to understand realities.*

The pause was short lived and in 1932, Stalin resumed his advance towards collectivization. Unfortunately, his decision coincided with a year of failed harvests and the famine affecting the Russian people intensified. In a forlorn hope that travellers might throw food from passing trains, desperate peasants waited along railway tracks. Mothers would go to any extreme to find small amounts of food for their children and there were those who even resorted to searching for grains in horse manure. In his book *Forever Flowing*, Vasily Grossman recalled what he had witnessed earlier with his own eyes.

> *The entire seed fund had been confiscated. Everywhere there was terror. Mothers looked at their children and screamed in fear. They screamed as if a snake had crept into their house. And this snake was famine, starvation, and death...And here, under the government of workers and peasants, not a grain was given them...Death from starvation mowed down the village. First the children, then the old people, then those of middle age. At first they dug graves and buried them, and then as things got worse they stopped. Dead people lay there in the yards and in the end remained in their huts. Things fell silent. The whole village died.*

The Ukraine, an area that once produced the most abundant harvests of grain, was one of the regions that offered the greatest resistance to collectivization and at one stage, Stalin even considered deporting the whole population. A remorseful officer in the OGPU commented:

> *I am an old Bolshevik. I worked in the underground against the Tsar and then fought in the civil war. Did I do all that in order that I should now surround villages with machine guns and order my men to fire indiscriminately into crowds of peasants? Oh no, no!*

As the confiscated grain was stockpiled, it was not used to feed the starving but sold abroad in order to earn much-needed foreign currency or allowed to rot and it was not uncommon to find wasted corpses lying outside fully stocked warehouses. Officially the government declared that there was no famine and for reasons of propaganda some collectives received additional government help to enable them to become showpiece Potemkin Villages. These would be used for showing to overseas visitors or newsreels intended for home consumption. It has been claimed that 10 million died but the chances are that it was very many more. Whatever, the number of both kulaks and peasants who perished places Stalin at the head of

those responsible for genocide and mass murder – even above
Adolf Hitler – and there was worse to come!

Just how successful was collectivization?

By 1925, about a quarter of Russian agricultural land was
collectively farmed and during the next 12 months this more than
doubled. By the mid-1930s, some 25 million peasant smallholdings
had been consolidated into 250,000 collective farms worked by
75 million people but the process was not completed until 1941,
the second year of the Soviet Union's involvement in the Second
World War. The chances of the success of collective farming were
not helped by excessive interference by government officials and
the fact that Party overseers were mainly inexperienced and often
incompetent. In addition, many peasants showed little enthusiasm
to work as wage labourers on land that they had once owned and
this was reflected in apathy and general decline. The *kolkhozee* were
Party run and payment to the workers was based on productivity so
if no profit was made, then there was no payout. Disenchantment
led to some 19 million rural workers leaving the countryside to
find employment in the new industrial areas. As we shall see, many
would have come to consider this a foolish move. Considered from
the point of view of production levels, collectivization proved little
short of a disaster.

After an initial impressive increase, the production of grain fell
slightly and by 1935 output had increased substantially (Table 4.1).
You will also notice that the number of animals fell dramatically
because many had been slaughtered rather than hand them over to
the collective farms and there was insufficient feed for animals during
the winter. It is also worthy of note that the number of horses in the
Soviet Union, 34 million in 1929, had fallen to 17 million by 1933.
This had an adverse effect since, although tractors were becoming
increasingly available, horses still played an essential role in
farm work.

In the end, collective farms, despite their inefficiency and
mismanagement, did begin to produce more grain. Still Stalin could
not have been impressed by the fact that the peasants were producing
more grain on their small private plots than the collectives! A cartoon
of the time showed well-fed peasants working amongst the luxuriant

Table 4.1   Agricultural production figures 1928–35

	1928	1929	1930	1931	1932	1933	1934	1935
Grain (million tonnes)	73.3	71.7	83.5	69.5	69.6	68.6	67.6	75.0
Cattle (million head)	70.5	67.1	52.5	47.9	40.7	38.4	42.4	49.3
Pigs (million head)	26.0	20.4	13.6	14.4	11.6	12.1	17.4	22.6
Sheep and goats (million head)	146.7	147.0	108.8	77.7	52.1	50.2	51.9	61.1

vegetables on their own private plot and sending their grandmother off to work on the collective. There was also the story that the state appointment official who ran a collective bought 1,000 chickens out of the collective's profits and promised that they could keep half once they were fully grown. Later he discovered that the majority of those returned were cockerels!

Although the amenities promised to those who lived on collective settlements were slow to appear, Communist propagandists went to great lengths to use photographs and paintings to show the idyllic lifestyle of the peasants employed on collectives. On the credit side, it must be remembered that collectivization brought with it the greater use of mechanization and the introduction of improved farming methods. Most importantly, in the end it created 250,000 *kolkhozee* that proved capable of supporting the growing population of the Soviet Union's expanding industrial regions. Of course, all this must be measured against the cost in terms of human life and misery as Stalin sacrificed the Russian peasantry to begin the economic transformation of his country.

5

Stalin's economic policies (2) – the Five-Year Plans

This chapter will cover:
- *Stalin's plans to industrialize Russia*
- *the theory of Five-Year Planning*
- *the achievements of the First, Second and Third Five-Year Plans*
- *the impact of the Plans on the industrial workers*
- *Stakhanovism*
- *Stalin's economic revolution – success or failure?*

> *We must transform the USSR from a weak, agrarian country dependent on the whims of world capitalism, drive out the capitalist elements mercilessly, widen the front of the socialist forms of the economy and create the economic basis for the construction of a socialist society...*
>
> From a speech made by Stalin when he introduced the First Five-Year Plan in 1928

Five-year planning

Next, Stalin embarked upon the really important aim of his economic reforms, a colossal programme of development that would transform the Soviet Union into an advanced industrial state capable of matching the country's capitalist neighbours. The programme was to be as ruthlessly enforced as collectivization. Basically, Five-Year Planning is a programme of staged development with set economic objectives set five years in advance.

Each industrial unit was to be set predetermined quotas, minimum amounts that had to be achieved over a five-year period, and each worker was set a weekly norm – a minimum amount that they were expected to produce. The scheme was backed by a system of rewards and punishments. Workers who managed to exceed their norms became entitled to extra pay, additional rations of food and, in the long run, improved housing and other additional benefits whilst those who failed to achieve their norms forfeited some of their pay and had the food to which they were entitled reduced. Of course, the OGPU was always at hand to deal with slackers: latecomers and those who complained were punished with additional hard labour. Absenteeism brought dismissal and this meant that the worker lost his home and entitlement to rations whilst any hint of sabotage or industrial espionage meant death. The overall supervision of the plans was placed in the hands of Gosudarstvenny Planovy Komitet, a State Planning Committee usually referred to by the acronym Gosplan. Based in Moscow, Gosplan employed over half a million officials whose job it was to set the targets for each factory, works and mine and then check that the targets set were actually achieved. The regimented workers, many of them unskilled or newly arrived from the countryside, were forced to endure the most appalling working and living conditions in which all safety regulations were ignored. Piecework – payment according to how much the worker produced – replaced time-rate – payment according to the number of hours worked – and a seven-day working week was introduced. Displayed everywhere were posters and slogans intended to urge the workers to even greater efforts as well as charts boasting of the production figures achieved. Fuel was short and many factories and homes were unheated even in the depths of a Russian winter. There were numerous instances when men and women broke down under the strain imposed upon them and some literally worked themselves to death.

Remember too that factory managers were made personally responsible for reaching their targets and those who failed faced the possibility of trial, punishment and even execution. On the other hand, although they received scant reward for their hard work, the majority set about the task of modernizing their country with dedication and great enthusiasm. Workers were assailed by all forms of propaganda whilst the young, who were idealistic, found the challenge of Communism intoxicating. State controlled trade unions also played their part in encouraging workers to increase productivity. An American, John Scott, who witnessed their efforts at first hand wrote:

> **They had their noses to the grindstone but they knew that it was for themselves, for a future with dignity and freedom for all workers. Strange as it may appear, the forced labour was a source not only of privation but also of heroism… Soviet youth found heroism in working in factories and on construction sites.**
>
> (*Behind the Urals: An American Worker in Russia's City of Steel* by John Scott, 1942)

Another American, who witnessed living conditions in workers' dormitories, saw things differently:

> **The room contained approximately 500 narrow beds covered with mattresses filled with straw or dried leaves. There were no pillows or blankets…some had no beds and slept on the floor or in wooden boxes…There were no screens or walls to give any privacy. There were no closets or wardrobes because each one only owned the clothing on his back.**
>
> *I Was A Soviet Worker* by Andrew Smith

In reality, Soviet men and women in the 1930s were willingly sacrificing their today for the benefit of future generations – their children and grandchildren.

The First Five-Year Plan, 1928–33

As Stalin strove to bring about an economic miracle, the emphasis of the First Five-Year Plan was placed on heavy industry, particularly the construction of factories to produce capital goods such as machinery, machine tools and tractors. In addition, dams had to be built to provide hydro-electric power and there would be a need to increase production and find new sources of essential raw materials, particularly iron, steel, coal and oil. The Plan was also intended to expand into new areas of production such as chemicals, motor vehicles, synthetic rubber and artificial fibres. To ensure adequate transport and communication facilities, there would also be a need to build additional roads, railways and canals. As factory managers and their workers struggled to cope with unrealistic quotas, there were some who pleaded for a slowing down in the stampede towards industrialization. Stalin's response was:

> *The pace must not be slackened! On the contrary, we must quicken it as much as is within our powers and possibilities. To slacken the pace would mean to lag behind, and those who lag behind are beaten.*

There was to be no respite and to add to the pressure, after a year Stalin decided to make even greater demands on the workers so that the Plan would be completed in four!

A Soviet propaganda poster of 1931 shows a capitalist first ridiculing the First Five-Year Plan and then wincing when it is completed in only four years.

Although this period of intense industrial activity brought no improvement in the living standards of the workers, it did provide the springboard for the continued economic development of the

Table 5.1   Production figures for the First Five-Year Plan (shown in millions of tonnes)

	1927–28 actual production	1928–33 target	1932 amended target	1933 actual production
Coal	35	75	95–105	64
Iron-ore	6.7	20.2	24–32	12.1
Pig iron	3.2	10	15–16	6.2
Oil	11.7	21.7	40–55	21.4

Soviet Union. The First Five-Year Plan was noted for some remarkable achievements such as the construction of a huge dam across the River Dnieper that increased the electricity supply by 600 per cent, the new steel works at Magnitogorsk, car factories at Moscow and Gorki and tractor factories at Rostov and Kharkov. Communications were improved with canals built to connect the White Sea with the Baltic and Moscow with the River Volga. The railway system was further extended and the magnificent Moscow metro completed. This underground system with its elegant, chandelier-lit platforms and marble-walled stations was considered the most spectacular achievement and exploited as a tourist attraction. However, as far as heavy industry was concerned, none of the original targets were achieved, let alone the revised targets set in 1932. Reliable statistics are difficult to come by since managers, fearing for their positions and even their lives, inflated their returns so that in many instances the figures claimed fell far short of the true production levels!

The Second Five-Year Plan, 1933–8

When it came to the Second Five-Year Plan, those who set the targets were far more realistic and with lower figures set, there was some relaxation and production went more smoothly. Stalin was still determined to concentrate on heavy industry and production figures improved. The first trickle of consumer goods, food, clothing and household products began to appear in the shops but in insufficient quantities and they always had to be queued for. There was little overall improvement in living conditions and the everyday lives of the workers and their families remained grim. Still, in 1935 bread rationing came to an end and other foodstuffs such as vegetables, meat, fats and sugar became more generally available. The deteriorating political situation in Europe, inflamed as it was by the rise to power of Hitler's Nazi Party in Germany, made Stalin aware of the need to place greater emphasis on defence and the production of armaments. Between 1933 and 1938, the production of armaments more than trebled and this placed an additional financial burden on the Soviet regime. A feature of the Second Five-Year Plan was the emergence of Stakhanovism.

Stakhanovism

On 1 September 1935, the Communist newspaper *Pravda* reported that a miner working in the Donets Basin had, on the 30–1 August, extracted 102 tonnes of coal in a single six-hour shift. His superhuman effort had achieved an output that was 14 times his expected norm! The man, Aleksey Grigorevich Stakhanov, had used his intelligence to introduce more effective working techniques including the division of labour so that his team of workers was able to increase its daily output sevenfold. The Communist Party acclaimed his achievement and it was used to motivate others through the encouragement of 'socialist competition'. Stakhanov and others who followed his example were rewarded with higher pay and other privileges such as free holidays, a chance to visit the Kremlin and the award of the Order of Lenin or Hero of Soviet Labour. Some workers even formed 'Shock Brigades' in an attempt to match Stakhanov's achievements. Instead of seeking to improve quality, Stakhanovism placed emphasis on speed and increased output at any price and this became the accepted norm. Outside Russia, trade union leaders criticized the Stakhanov movement since they regarded it as a none-too subtle way of exploiting workers. The movement also had its critics within the Soviet Union. Considered an elitist group, Stakhanovites attracted the resentment of others since their achievements increased the pressure on other workers to produce similar results. They were shunned, attacked and some, so it was claimed, murdered. Sceptics wonder if the miner's output was ever actually achieved and some even doubt if Stakhanov really existed and suggest that he was artificially created to assume the role of a workers' idol. In face of such opposition, Stakhanovism gradually lapsed but for the record, another miner, Nikita Isotov, later claimed to have mined over twice as much as Stakhanov in a single shift!

The Third Five-Year Plan, 1938–42

In 1938, the Eighteenth Party Conference approved the introduction of Stalin's Third Five-Year Plan. With German foreign policy becoming increasingly aggressive and the future peace of Europe under threat, the Soviet leadership made a further increase in arms production a top priority. Once again, the hopes of the Russian people of enjoying improved living standards based on a higher level of production of consumer goods were dashed and the years of austerity continued. After only three years, in June 1941, the Plan was interrupted by the German invasion of the Soviet Union and the country was plunged into war – the Second World War or, as it was known in Russia, the Great Patriotic War.

How successful was Stalin's economic revolution?

In assessing the success of the Five-Year Plans it is necessary to bear in mind that Soviet statistics were influenced by the needs of propaganda and the returns made by Gosplan were often greatly inflated. The estimates by Western economists of production levels are usually very much lower than those published by the official Soviet authorities. As a British trade union leader cynically commented, 'I read some time ago of Russian bricklayers who laid from 10,000 to 25,000 bricks in seven hours. The larger figure would mean that the workmen would have to lay one brick per second. My impression is that British bricks are larger than the Russian is!' It is also necessary to remember that Stalin brought in experts from overseas countries to help and advise in production methods and, by appointing individual factory managers, he abandoned one of Lenin's beliefs that factories should be run according to joint decisions made by workers' councils. The Five-Year Plans also suffered serious flaws. Parts needed to repair worn-out machinery were sometimes delayed or unavailable and this meant that workers were left idle for weeks on end. Many of the so-called skilled workers were in fact former peasants who had moved to the industrial regions from the countryside. This meant that machinery was liable to be damaged

Table 5.2   Comparison: Industrial Growth in Tsarist Russia and the Soviet Union

	1900	1913	1928	1932	1938	1940
Coal (m. tonnes)	20	19	34	62	130	166
Iron and steel (m. tonnes)	3	4	8	12	31	33
Oil (m.tonnes)	4	9	12	22	31	31
Electricity (m.watts)	0	80	1,000	5,000	11,000	13,000
Tractors	0	0	1,200	49,000	52,000	31,000

simply because they had no idea how to use it! Nevertheless, the years of the Five-Year Plans by any measurement represent a period of remarkable achievement and growth financed, as they were, entirely by the Russian people without the help of foreign loans. In spite of the country's trials and tribulations, during this period of rapid industrialization the population of the Soviet Union increased from 147 million to 170 million. By 1940, the USSR had overtaken Britain in the production of iron and steel and was close to catching up with Germany. As with collectivization, there was a price to pay as the people suffered shortages, low living standards, a loss of personal liberties and harassment by OGPU and Party officials. It would be fair to say that the majority of Russian workers were no better off in 1940 than they had been in 1920 and those who came originally from bourgeoisie backgrounds, very much worse. The success of industrialization should not hide the cost in human life and misery. Many of the new factories were built to the east of the Ural Mountains by slave labourers, those who had resisted collectivization and were now being 're-educated'. Their working conditions were gruesome and they were undernourished and lived in tents where large numbers died of exposure. It is impossible to accurately assess the number that died but estimates have been put at between 4 and 10 million.

6

From Marxism-Leninism to Stalinism

This chapter will cover:
* *the meaning of Stalinism*
* *the new constitution of 1936*
* *the Church and religion in Soviet Russia*
* *socialist realism and its impact on Soviet art and culture.*

> *O great Stalin, O leader of the peoples,*
> *Thou who broughtest man to birth.*
> *Thou, splendour of my spring, O thou,*
> *Sun reflected by millions of hearts...*

From a poem that appeared in *Pravda* in February 1935

Introduction

The basic ideas of socialism – the establishment of a classless society, a change from private to public ownership of the means of production and distribution – existed long before Karl Marx. Socialist ideas appeared in the writings of Greek and Roman scholars, in early Christianity, amongst later Christian sects such as the seventeenth-century Levellers, and in the writings of the Frenchmen Jean-Jacques Rousseau, Claude Saint-Simon and Francois Fourier. In the early nineteenth century, a Welshman, Robert Owen, set up a model community at New Lanark in Scotland and proposed the idea of 'villages of co-operation' run on socialist lines. However, it was the German-born political philosophers and social theorists, Karl Marx and Friedrich Engels, whose ideas were to have such a profound influence on nineteenth- and twentieth-century political thinkers and revolutionary activists. Marx put forward a theory known as dialectical materialism which, applied to history, supposes that economic and social development passes through successive stages of feudalism, capitalism and socialism before inevitably creating a classless society. Each stage would be an improvement on its predecessor and the final stage would only be reached after a class struggle during which the capitalist system would be overthrown and replaced by a dictatorship of the working class, the proletariat. Marx's famous battle cry to the working classes appeared in his Communist Manifesto of 1848:

> *...a spectre is haunting Europe – the spectre of communism... the history of all hitherto existing society is the history of class struggles...Let the ruling classes tremble at a communist revolution. The proletarians have nothing to lose but their chains. They have a world to win. Workers of the world unite.*

Marx died in 1883 and although his lifetime witnessed major upheavals in Europe – 1848, a 'Year of Revolutions' and the emergence of Italy and Germany as nation states – he did not live long enough to see his theories applied to the management of the economic, political and social life of the world's first communist country. In fact, Marx spent most of his latter years living in Britain and there is some irony in the fact that he lies buried in Highgate Cemetery in London, one of the world's major centres of capitalist activity!

Marxism – the Russian experience

From a Marxist point of view, in the nineteenth century the problem with Russia was that it was still a semi-feudal, peasant society with only a small urban-based proletariat. It was the gradual industrialization of the country that helped to create circumstances more favourable to the spread of Marxist propaganda. The true 'Father of Russian Marxism' was Georgi Plekhanov who helped to found the first Marxist organization in Russia, the Emancipation of Labour group. He later joined the Social Democrats and when the party split, became a Menshevik. Hounded by the tsarist secret police, he fled abroad and only returned in 1917. In the meantime, the responsibility for spreading Marxism had passed to intellectuals such as Lenin and Trotsky. After the revolution of 1917 and a successful outcome to the civil war that followed, Lenin adapted Marxist principles to what he judged to be in the best interests of the Russian people and so produced an ideology known as Marxism-Leninism. He intended to push through policies needed to ensure the speedy transition of the country from capitalism to socialism. In his book, *Das Kapital*, Marx had warned of the difficulties that lay ahead when he wrote: 'The evils of a capitalist society cannot be abolished by reform...but only by the destruction of the whole capitalist economy and the establishment of a new classless society'. As we have seen, once in power Lenin took it upon himself to work towards achieving Marx's aim, an egalitarian society free from all capitalist influences. At first, Stalin went along with the old Marxism-Leninism and people spoke of Marxist-Leninist-Stalinist principles but as his position became more secure, so he began to encourage, not just a shift in emphasis, but a fundamental change in the direction of policies affecting Russian economic, political and social life. These represented a move towards what was to become known solely as Stalinism. As we shall see, Stalinism came to represent a hotchpotch of ideologies and this makes a clear definition difficult.

Stalinism

You will remember that Stalin had rejected Trotsky's view that socialism could not thrive in a single country and that the survival of a Russian communist state depended on the success of proletarian revolutions in other European countries. From the start, he was convinced that a socialist society could be created within a single country even though that country was isolated and surrounded by hostile capitalist states. Neither did Stalin hesitate to challenge or even reverse the previously accepted doctrines of Marxism-Leninism. His drive to enforce his Five-Year Plans on Russia was based on what he identified as the need to create a modern industrial state able to produce the military wherewithal to survive in a largely hostile capitalist world. Amongst the first to be rejected was the old Marxist principle 'from each according to his ability, to each according to his needs' since to encourage the workers, Stalin found it necessary to agree wage differentials and offer bonus incentives.

Rapid industrialization created a shortage of engineers and draftsmen and this caused Stalin to reject the old Marxist view that workers required only a basic education. To cover the shortfall, he provided more opportunities for able students to benefit from a technical or university education.

In schools, there was a return to more formal teaching methods and far stricter discipline enforced and whilst Marxist-Leninists had considered marriage to be bourgeois and outdated, Stalin urged a return to family values and encouraged marriage. Divorce was made more difficult and abortion declared illegal. Again, according to Marxism-Leninism, crime was supposed to 'wither away' with the development of a socialist state but since the country was experiencing a crime wave, Stalin did not hesitate to introduce a new penal code with more severe punishments for criminal behaviour. He also reversed the decision to abolish rank and the wearing of insignia in the armed forces. Some of the measures introduced, particularly higher wages linked to bonuses and a new emphasis on higher education, led to the creation of a new breed of highly qualified and well paid men and women. Such people, mainly engineers, scientists, doctors and teachers, appeared to enjoy all the trappings of the old bourgeoisie and from their ranks were to come the new Party functionaries and bureaucrats needed to replace the former Leninist elite, the Old Bolsheviks. Sadly, these changes represented only one aspect of Stalinism. There was another.

Whereas traditional Marxists believed that the State would decline as socialism developed, Stalin held the view that the State had to become stronger to cope with the many challenges faced by socialism. As part of his drive to establish 'socialism in one country', he had imposed collectivization and rapid industrialization on the country and backed this up with the use of terror needed to intimidate the people. From 1936, the Soviet leader imposed his personal dictatorship on the people through the use of a secret police whose excesses even surpassed those of the tsarist *Okhrana*. In the end, Stalin would not tolerate any challenge to his authority and gone was the idea that one day the Soviet Union would be democratically governed by an elected collective leadership. As we shall see, Stalin's dictatorship extended beyond the fields of politics and economics into culture and religion and affected every aspect of the lives of ordinary Russian people.

Definitions of Stalinism are as numerous and varied as the number of historians who have written about the Soviet leader. Stephen F. Cohen describes Stalinism as:

> *not simply nationalism, bureaucratization, absence of democracy, censorship, police repression...These phenomena have appeared in many societies and are rather easily explained. Indeed Stalinism was excess, extraordinary extremism, in each...Excesses...are what really require explanation.*
>
> *Bolshevism and Stalinism* by Stephen F. Cohen, 1980

The Australian historian, Graeme Gill, expresses the view that Stalinism was:

> *A personal dictatorship, resting upon the use of terror as an instrument of rule and in which the political institutions are little more than the instrument of the dictator.*
>
> *Stalinism* by Graeme Gill, 1975

Martin McCauley comments:

> *Stalinism was demotic but not democratic, and pitiless in subjecting men and women to material goals. The needs of the State and the economy took precedence over every private desire. Stalin, by 1941, had mown down the harvest of potential opponents and left himself as the only stalk standing.*
>
> *The Soviet Union Since 1917* by Martin McCauley, 1981

Put rather more simply, Stalin's reign was one of terror and oppression and his ideology, Stalinism, reflected this!

Stalin's 'cult of personality'

One of the features of Stalin's rule was the development of a 'cult of personality'. The term 'cult of personality' refers to the excessive adulation of a person and is usually applied to the leader of a totalitarian state. It is normally made evident by the fact that the leader's pictures appear everywhere, as do statues and monuments proclaiming his greatness and wisdom. Massive posters displaying his popular slogans and books containing his speeches and writings are readily available in bookshops. Stalin could bestow no greater honour on a town or city than allow it to be renamed after him and this gave rise to Stalinabad, Stalino, Stalinsk and, of course, Stalingrad. Stalin's propagandists also saw to it that nothing from his past would besmirch the Soviet leader's image. Stories about his childhood and early years were enhanced and new ones fabricated and earlier pictures taken of Stalin with disgraced Old Bolsheviks were altered so that they became obvious, crude forgeries. The historian David King has described this as 'pictorial genocide'. To outsiders, such adulation and flattery seemed absurd and the term 'cult of personality' came to be used in a derogatory sense. Stalin liked to present himself as a humble and modest man and dismissed the idolization as nothing more than a spontaneous show of affection by the Russian people.

To sustain his 'cult of personality', artists, musicians and writers were only allowed to produce works that further embellished his image. There can be no greater evidence of fawning adulation than the poem that appeared in the Russian newspaper, *Pravda*, in 1934:

> *O great Stalin, O leader of the peoples,*
> *Thou who broughtest man to birth.*
> *Thou who fructifiest* the earth,*
> *Thou who restorist the centuries,*
> *Thou who makest bloom the spring,*
> *Thou who makest vibrate the musical chords,*
> *Thou, splendour of my spring, O Thou,*
> *Sun reflected by millions of hearts...*

*To fructify means to make fruitful.

In 1939, Nikita Khrushchev, a delegate to the Eighteenth Party Congress, said:

> *Every Bolshevik, every worker, every citizen of our Soviet land is clearly aware that if we had been able to route all these fascist agents, all these contemptible Trotskyists, Bucharinists and bourgeois nationalists, we are indebted to our great leader, our great and glorious Stalin.*

Seventeen years later and three years after the death of the Soviet leader, the same man made a speech at the Twentieth Party Conference that triggered the destruction of the Stalin legend!

Stalin's new constitution of 1936

In 1933, the Soviet Union was made up of 11 republics that were each divided into administrative units known as *oblasts* (*oblastey*) or provinces and autonomous regions known as *okrugs* (*okrugov*) with smaller units or districts called *rayons*.

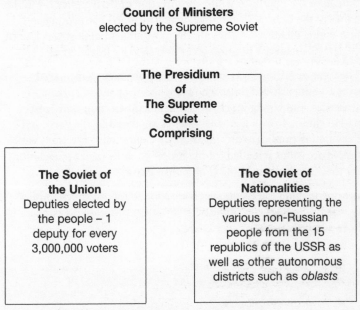

Figure 6.1 The Government of the Soviet Union based on the constitution of 1936.

The government of the country was based on a pyramid of Soviets. Under Stalin's proposed new constitution that was intended to replace that of 1924, the law-making body of the Union of Soviet Socialist Republics was to consist of two houses of equal authority – the Soviet of the Union and the Soviet of Nationalities. The Soviet of the Union contained 750 elected deputies whilst the Soviet of Nationalities was composed of 630 members drawn from the republics, other autonomous regions and nationalities that made up the Soviet Union. The two houses elected the 33 members of the all-important Presidium of the Supreme Soviet, with the president of the Presidium being regarded as the head of state.

At regional level, each republic elected its own Soviet, as did the smaller administrative regions. In reality, the Supreme Soviet existed mainly to approve the legislation placed before it by the secretariat of the Communist Party and since the Communist Party of the Soviet Union was the only legal political party, it was there that the real power lay.

Within the Party, the main decision-making body was the Political Bureau or the Politburo whilst the direction of Party policy lay in the hands of the Central Committee, which included both voting and non-voting members. Above all, the most influential post was that of General Secretary, a position invariably held by Josef Stalin!

The right of suffrage was extended to all men and women aged over 18 but excluded those who were insane or serving prison sentences, and voting was by secret ballot. At election time, voters had to choose from a list of candidates approved by the Party and the winning candidate was invariably a Communist. Elections were festive occasions intended for the people to show their appreciation for the achievements of the Communist Party.

Bearing in mind the events that were soon to follow, much implied in many of the Articles of the new Soviet Constitution may appear to have a hollow ring.

Some articles included in the new Soviet Constitution

Article 1	The Union of the Soviet Socialist Republics is a socialist state of workers and peasants.
Article 3	In the USSR all power belongs to the working people of town and country as represented by the soviets of Working People's Deputies.
Article 4	The socialist system of economy and the socialist ownership of the means of production...and the abolition of the exploitation of man by man, constitute the economic foundation of the USSR.

Article 6	The land, its natural deposits, waters, forests, mills... banks, post, telegraph...belong to the whole people.
Article 10	The right of citizens to personal ownership of their incomes from work and of their savings, of their dwelling houses, their household furniture...is protected by law.
Article 12	In the USSR work is a duty and a matter of honour for every able-bodied citizen in accordance with the principle, 'He who does not work neither shall he eat'.
Article 118	Citizens of the USSR have the right to work...
Article 119	Citizens of the USSR have the right to rest and leisure....
Article 120	Citizens of the USSR have the right of maintenance in old age and also in the case of sickness or loss of capacity to work.
Article 121	Citizens of the USSR have the right to education.
Article 122	Women in the USSR are accorded equal rights with men...
Article 124	...freedom of religious worship and freedom of anti-religious propaganda is recognized for all citizens.
Article 125	...citizens of the USSR are guaranteed by law: freedom of speech; freedom of the press; freedom of assembly; freedom to hold processions and demonstrations.
Article 127	No person can be put under arrest except by the decision of a court or with the sanction of the procurator.
Article 132	Universal military service is law.
Article 133	...Treason to the country and sabotage...are punishable with all the severity of the law as the most heinous of crimes.

Stalinism and religion

A Jew by birth, Karl Marx described religion as 'the sign of an oppressed creature, the feelings of a heartless world and the spirit of conditions which are unspiritual. It is the opium of the people.' In equating religion with a drug, Marx was expressing the view that religion, like a drug, allowed people to escape the pain of the harshness of their drab, everyday lives. He also believed that the ruling class had used religion to their own advantage by deluding the working classes into accepting their lowly status in life as the station 'into which God had called them'. The reward for their earthly suffering came with the promise of life after death in heaven. He also pointed out that the churches held great influence over the people, possessed great wealth and were themselves a 'pillar of the establishment' and part of the ruling class. Lenin's views were identical since he regarded religion as 'one of the forms of spiritual oppression which everywhere weigh heavily upon the masses of the people crushed by continuous toil for others, by poverty and loneliness…'.

Marx, however, favoured religious tolerance and was opposed to the persecution of the people for their religious beliefs and, as we have seen, Article 124 of the new 1936 constitution guaranteed freedom of worship. Nevertheless, after the Revolution the Bolsheviks began a campaign to stamp out religious practice. Their immediate targets were the Russian Orthodox Church and other Christian sects such as Baptists, Methodists, Lutherans and Seventh Day Adventists and they also turned their attention to the Jews as well as Muslims and Buddhists who lived in their Asian republics. During the Civil War, priests and their congregations suffered at the hands of the Bolsheviks and in 1929, a law was passed that made it illegal to hold religious ceremonies outside church buildings and buildings used for religious worship had to be licensed. You will remember that during his youth, Stalin's mother set him on the path to becoming a priest but he left the seminary and instead he embraced Marxism and atheism. During the period of collectivization and industrialization, the situation worsened considerably. Accused of being capitalist agents and in league with the kulaks, priests were arrested and murdered and their churches closed. Many church leaders were to fall victims of Bolshevik terror and 28 bishops and over 1,200 priests were executed. In addition, the Bible was banned, icons destroyed, theological colleges closed and church valuables confiscated.

Muslims were not allowed to follow Islamic Law and fasting during the Holy Month of Ramadan was forbidden. Women could no longer wear the veil and men were banned from joining pilgrimages to Mecca.

A League of the Militant Godless was founded in 1923 to promote atheism and orchestrate a campaign against religion, particularly the

Russian Orthodox Church. Anti-religious propaganda that appeared in two magazines, *Bezbozhnik* (Godless) and *Antireligioznik* (Anti-Religious Worker) helped to popularize the work of the League. As part of the attack on church institutions, marriage became a civil ceremony and a dim view was taken of the wearing of wedding rings. Cremation of the dead was encouraged rather than burial, the religious observance of Sunday abandoned and religious instruction in schools was abolished to be replaced by anti-religious teaching and the setting up of anti-religious museums. Those who persisted with their religious beliefs became the objects of mockery and abuse and were sometimes physically attacked whilst within the Party: a good Communist was of necessity an atheist. Briefly, during 1935, Stalin's campaign against religion eased and for a while Easter novelties and Christmas trees reappeared, priests were better treated and a number of churches reopened. However, with the start of the Terror, the campaign against religion was once again renewed. In spite of all the persecution, it is estimated that over half the Russian people continued to actively support the Church. In order to survive, the Church went underground and priests abandoned their clerical robes to conduct religious services in secret. In 1941, the Communist anti-religion campaign was abandoned and Stalin went as far as to appeal to the Church to support the country's war effort against Germany.

Anti-Semitism was not new to Russia since in tsarist times, the persecution and unprovoked massacres of Jews were regular occurrences. Known as *pogroms* – *pogrom* is a Russian word that means devastation – those that followed the assassination of Alexander II in 1881, a crime for which Jews were held responsible, were particularly vicious and led to a mass emigration of thousands of Russian Jews, mainly to the United States. Another series of *pogroms* between 1903 and 1906 led to the killing and wounding of hundreds of Russian Jews whilst the authorities did nothing to prevent the systematic pillaging of their homes and businesses. In spite of the fact that many leading Bolsheviks were of Jewish extraction – Trotsky, Bukharin, Kamenev and Zinoviev – after the Revolution, Russian Jewry was persecuted with the closure of their schools, libraries and synagogues and a ban placed on the study of Hebrew. In Stalinist Russia, anti-Semitism was never far beneath the surface and Judaism was attacked as part of the general assault on religion. Yet elsewhere in Europe, the number of revolutionaries of Jewish origin gave credence to the widely held belief that

Communism was a Jewish-Bolshevik conspiracy! As far as Russian Jews were concerned, the worst period of blatant anti-Semitism was still to come.

Stalin's 'cultural revolution'

Although the events of 1917 had caused many Russian writers, artists and musicians to flee abroad, it was the hope of those that remained that the post-revolutionary period would allow them to enjoy greater freedom of expression than before. Lenin had expressed the view that access to the arts should be freely available to all and the early 1920s was certainly a period of creativity in all forms of the arts. *Narkompros*, the People's Commissariat for Enlightenment, not only took over the art galleries and museums but arranged for new ones to be built. However, once Stalin was in power, all forms of creative art were directed towards *partiinost* – serving the needs of the Communist Party. His aim was to bring about a 'cultural revolution' that would serve the needs of Stalinism.

Under the Communist regime, writers who hoped to get their works published had to join the Association of Proletarian Writers, the *Rossiiskaya Assotsiatsiya Proletarskikh Pisatelei* or RAPP. The Association, described as representing 'the elite troops of the cultural revolution', sought to eliminate bourgeois thinking and urged writers to concentrate on the lives and achievements of the proletariat. So the period produced literature described by Martin McCauley as 'the glorification of the man in the street'. RAPP was short lived and in 1932, accused of impatience and vulgar socialism, it was abolished and replaced by the Union of Soviet Writers. The Union imposed on writers a new political correctness that had to accord with socialist realism. The man who set down the cultural rules and promoted socialist realism was Andrei Zhdanov, who had earlier succeeded Kirov as Party leader in Leningrad.

LITERATURE

According to Stalin, writers now had to be 'engineers of human souls' and had to ensure that their works showed *partiinost*, party mindedness, and the language used in their books was easily accessible to the average worker. Socialist realism also represented a change from writing about the proletariat to describing the achievements of collectivization, the achievements of the Five-Year Plans and the glorification of Stalin. It also marked a reversal of the earlier Bolshevik view that past history was irrelevant with a rediscovery of the national heroes of Russian history as writers were again encouraged to examine the lives of such as Ivan the Terrible, Peter the Great and Catherine the Great. Amongst the famous Soviet writers of the time were Maxim Gorki, Mikhail Sholokhov and Aleksandr Fadeyev.

Maxim Gorki was the pen name of Alexsei Peshkov who spent the early years of his life living as a down and out or by taking part-time manual jobs. These experiences later provided him with the material for his novels and plays. He first became famous as a writer in tsarist times but following his arrest for his involvement in revolutionary activities, he spent much of his time living abroad. Although a close friend of Lenin, Gorki was opposed to the armed seizure of power by the Bolsheviks in 1917 and between 1921 and 1928, he lived in Mussolini's fascist Italy but then returned to Russia to help develop the idea of socialist realism. He died in 1936 whilst undergoing medical treatment but there are those who suspect that he was murdered on Stalin's orders since he was clearly changing his mind about the policies being followed by the Communist regime. After his death, his birthplace, Nizhni Novgorod was renamed Gorki in his honour.

After serving in the Red Army during the Civil War, Mikhail Sholokhov was reduced to supporting himself by doing manual work. In 1925, he published his first book, *Tales of the Don*, which was an account of the suffering of a family during the Civil War. Sholokhov did not join the Communist Party until 1932 and in 1937 he was elected to the Supreme Soviet. During the 1930s, some Party members thought him guilty of treason when he was openly critical of the treatment of the kulaks and the mass arrests that accompanied the purges but Stalin saw to it that he was spared. By far his most successful book was *And Quiet Flows the Don*, published in 1934. The four-volume book that covered events in the Soviet Union during the period 1928–40 became immensely popular and, considered a masterpiece, sold millions of copies in Russia and abroad. In 1941, Sholokhov was awarded the Stalin Prize for Literature. Later, the Russian dissident, Aleksandr Solzhenitsyn, alleged that *And Quiet Flows the Don* had been plagiarized from the works of a little known

Cossack writer! Aleksandr Fadeyev, who is barely known outside Russia, is most famous for his *The Nineteen* and *The Last of the Udegs*, a novel set in the Civil War. From 1939 to 1953, he was the secretary of the Union of Soviet Writers and was so moved by Stalin's death in 1956 that he committed suicide.

Amongst the writers to flee the country was Vladimir Nabokov, the son of a former liberal politician who, in turn, lived in Berlin, Paris and New York. His most famous book, *Lolita*, was published in 1955.

ART

Art, particularly modern art, did not get off to a good start when in 1920, Lenin declared himself to be 'a barbarian who disliked Expressionism, Futurism, Cubism and all other isms'. He was also critical of the limited appeal and elitism of art when he said, 'it does not matter what art gives to hundreds or even thousands, out of a population numbering millions. Art belongs to the people'. In spite of these views, for a time after the Revolution modern art was allowed to flourish until the Ministry of Culture imposed the traditionalism demanded by socialist realism. As a result, many of the country's leading artists including Natalia Goncharova, Vasilii Kandinsky and Konstantin Korov moved abroad. Henceforward, artists had to portray people, scenes and events as they really were and could not produce abstracts. The abstract artists who remained had their work condemned and it was never exhibited. The leading Russian artists of the day were Ivor Grabar and Konstantin Iuon who both painted revolutionary scenes and were recognized as People's Artists of the Soviet Union. Vasilii Baksheev, a representative of the older generation of Russian artists, agreed to toe the line of realist art as did the former painter of religious subjects, Mikhail Nesterov, who became a master portrait painter. Other accomplished artists had to be content to paint posters that illustrated the achievements of Russian communism. The main direction of Soviet sculpture was towards creating impressive works depicting aspects of the Revolution and Civil War, but there were outstanding sculptors such as Vera Mukhina who created delicate ornamental statuettes.

ARCHITECTURE

Socialist realism demanded that Soviet architecture be more functional than beautiful. In major Russian cities, 'wedding cake' type skyscrapers appeared, the most famous being the Moscow State University and the Ministry of Foreign Affairs. In order to provide sufficient dwellings for a rapidly growing urban population, large blocks of high-rise flats – 'boring monoliths' – were built. Although each flat was intended to provide a minimum living space of 4.66 square metres per person, there was chronic overcrowding with families forced to live in a single room. One of the country's most famous architects, Alexic Shchusev, was responsible for 'a masterpiece of architectural simplicity', Lenin's Mausoleum in Moscow's Red Square just outside the walls of the Kremlin. Intended to hold the embalmed body of their former leader, it was originally made of wooden cubes but in 1930 red granite cubes that formed a pyramid replaced these.

MUSIC

Following the Revolution in 1917, there was an exodus of Russia's most gifted composers and musicians. Those that chose to leave included Nicolai Medtner, Sergei Rachmaninov, Igor Stravinsky, Nicolai and Alexander Tcherepnin and Sergei Prokofiev.

Famous musicians who fled the Soviet Union

Nicolai Medtner

A gifted composer and pianist who was most famous for his piano sonatas. He left Russia in 1921 to settle first in France and then in Britain, where he died in 1951.

Sergei Prokofiev

During the First World War, he was excused military service in order to continue with his musical studies. After the war, he went into self-imposed exile but returned to the Soviet Union in 1935. His most famous work was *Peter and the Wolf*.

Sergei Rachmaninov

Studied at the St Petersburg and Moscow Conservatories and became a famous composer, pianist and conductor. Left Russia in 1917 to become one of the most distinguished pianists of his day. His most famous works include his second piano concerto and the *Rhapsody on a Theme of Paganini*. He made his home in the United States and died there in 1943.

Igor Stravinsky

Son of a singer with the Imperial Opera, he was a student of Rimsky-Korsakov before working with the ballet impresario Sergei Diaghilev. He left Russia in 1921 to make his home in the United States. His most famous works include *The Fire Bird* and *The Rite of Spring*.

Nicolai and Alexander Tcherepnin

Father and son were both gifted composers and pianists. They left Russia after the Revolution and settled in Paris. Nicolai Tcherepnin's most famous work was *The Dance of the Red Death* whilst his son composed chamber music.

Second-generation descendants of earlier Russian émigrés were to include Leonard Bernstein whose family left Russia in 1917 to make their home in the United States. Conductor of the New York Philharmonic Symphony Orchestra, he is most famous for the Broadway hit musical, *West Side Story*. The pianist and conductor, Daniel Barenboim, is also the son of Russian Jewish emigrants.

Composers who remained had to belong to the Composers' Union and their works had to conform to socialist realism and have 'a socialist content and be expressed in a musical language that ordinary people could easily understand'. Alexander Mossolov's symphony the *Iron Foundry* certainly had socialist content since it included all sorts of industrial sounds and was described by Gilbert Seldes as 'music…closely associated to pile driving, electric dynamos and rapid transit'. Certainly avant-garde, Mossolov got away with it because he described the symphony as being 'socialist realist music' but his good fortune did not last. In 1938, the composer was arrested, charged with being drunk and behaving lewdly, sent to a labour camp and removed from the Composer's Union. Other music thought to be too avant-garde and consequently unacceptable were the works of most modern composers and degenerate American 'swing' and 'jazz'.

After living abroad, in 1935 Sergei Prokofiev returned home and resumed his Russian citizenship. His most famous works were *Peter and the Wolf* and the score for the film *Alexander Nevsky* but it is likely that he was never forgiven for his earlier indiscretion of choosing to live abroad and, at a composers' conference in 1948, he was heavily censured for excessive originality. Another noted Soviet composer, Dmitry Shostakovich, was also criticized for failing to uphold the principles of socialist realism and he was ordered to simplify his style. However, his patriotic *Leningrad Symphony* of 1941, written to glorify the heroic defence of the city when encircled by the Germans, restored him to favour and he was awarded the Order of the Red Banner. Although *Song of Stalin* won great acclaim for the Armenian composer, Aram Khachaturian, the fact that he showed a certain independence of style irritated Soviet officials. Many years later, his most famous work, *Sabre Dance*, made the pop charts in Britain! Interestingly, after the Revolution the *Internationale* was adopted as the Soviet national anthem but in 1944 Alexandr Alexandrov's *Hymn of the Soviet People* replaced it.

BALLET

Of all the arts, Russia was best known for the quality of its ballet. The worldwide fame of Moscow's Bolshoi Ballet Company and the Academic Theatre in Leningrad, later renamed the Kirov Ballet after the assassination of the city's Party leader, together with the reputation of such dancers as Anna Pavlova and Galina Ulanova, allowed this to continue in Soviet times. Even so, the greatest of all impresarios, Sergei Diaghilev, never returned to Russia after 1917 and his famous *Ballets Russes* never appeared in the Soviet Union. The legendary dancer, Vaslav Nijinsky, was declared insane and lived abroad until his death in London in 1919 whilst Russia's famous choreographer, Mathilde Kschessinskaya, who was married to Tsar Nicholas II's cousin, also wisely left the country.

CINEMA

Lenin, who described film making as 'the most important art', fully recognized the value of the cinema as a means of indoctrinating and educating the masses. Although the cinema was still in its infancy and the films were silent and in black and white, films presented the Bolsheviks with a unique opportunity of encouraging the people to share their ideals. As with other arts, the Revolution saw many of Russia's film-makers fleeing from the country and this meant that a new generation of young film-makers had to be found who shared the Party's vision. Of course, the Soviet film industry had to follow the official style, socialist realism. An outstanding if controversial Russian film-maker and a man still recognized as one of the greatest directors of all time was Sergei Eisenstein. Born in Riga in Latvia in 1881, he first trained to be a civil engineer before serving in the Red Army during the Civil War. Given the job of re-establishing the Soviet film industry, his first film, *Strike*, made in 1924, firmly established his reputation. The film, which described the brutal methods used by the authorities to end a strike, was considered a brilliant piece of Communist propaganda. By far his most famous film *The Battleship Potemkin* was made the following year and is now considered a classic. It covered the events of a naval mutiny in 1905 (see Chapter 2). His films were noted for their realism and brilliantly taken close-ups. Eisenstein's later films included *Alexander Nevski* and *Ivan the Terrible*. Also important to the Russian film industry were Vsevoled Pudovkin and Dziga Vertov. Pudovkin not only made films but also wrote books on film-making technique whilst Vertov was famous for his newsreels, *Kino-Pravda*, which were used to promote socialist realism. The content of films had to be approved by the Party and the films had to be readily understood by largely uneducated audiences. To ensure that the films had the greatest impact, they were regularly shown in villages and in specially adapted trains that toured the countryside.

CIRCUSES

Being easy to understand and more egalitarian in its appeal, the circus was considered on a par with ballet and opera in the Soviet Union. However, few appreciate that it was a Newcastle-under-Lyme born Englishman, Philip Astley, who, in the late eighteenth century, first introduced the circus to Russia. They were to become extremely popular and in Stalinist Russia a circus school was established in Moscow to produce trained performers who 'walked tightropes, did back flips and stomped around in big floppy shoes from Minsk to Murmansk'.

THE MEDIA

The two leading Russian newspapers were *Pravda* (Truth) and *Izvestia* (News). Founded in tsarist times, after the October Revolution *Pravda* became the official newspaper of the Bolshevik Party whilst *Izvestia* first appeared in 1917. The official Soviet news agency, TASS, was set up in 1925 and was intended to provide news coverage for the whole country. TASS was to have correspondents spread across the whole of the Soviet Union and abroad but many were known NKVD (secret police) agents. When they first came to power, the Bolsheviks closed down all the newspapers and printing presses to prevent counter-revolutionaries 'poisoning the masses'. Claiming that the move was temporary, the first Soviet constitution of 1918 confirmed the confiscation of the printing presses and their transfer to the proletariat. Whilst the constitution of 1936 guaranteed the freedom of the press, this was only on condition that it 'coincided with the interests of the workers and served to strengthen the socialist order'.

To Lenin, the most effective way of communicating with the Soviet people was by means of the radio. He said:

> *Every village should have a radio. Every government office as well as every club in our factories should be aware that at a certain hour they will hear political news and the major events of the day.*

This was easier said than done since radio receivers were very expensive and not yet available to the general public. In 1918, the control of the limited broadcasting facilities that existed passed to the People's Commissariat for Posts and Telegraphs.

7

Stalin's terror – a time of purges and show trials

This chapter will cover:
- *early episodes and trials*
- *the consequences of the assassination of Serge Kirov*
- *the great purges and show trials*
- *the roles of Yagoda, Yezhov and Vyshinsky*
- *the fate of Trotsky.*

> *Cruelty has a human heart,*
> *And jealousy a human face;*
> *Terror the human form divine,*
> *And secrecy the human dress.*

(William Blake, 1757–1827)

From bloodless revolution to terror and mass murder

The bloodless revolution of October 1917 may have given the Russian people hope of a more peaceful and less taxing future but this was not to be the case. The use of terror was not new and many still retained bitter memories of tsarist times – the atrocities committed by the *Okhrana*, and the mass executions and deportations to Siberia. As we have seen during the years of War Communism, Lenin was prepared to use a Cheka-backed 'Red Terror' to eliminate those who opposed his policies and those he didn't trust. Stalin had employed 'a red holocaust' to exterminate the kulaks who opposed his policy of collectivization and then imposed a most severe regime on the Russian people as they struggled to achieve the often impossible targets of his Five-Year Plans but far worse was to follow! During the late 1920s, a series of trials took place involving specialist workers who were either foreign or came from bourgeois backgrounds. They were accused of treason, acts of espionage and working to restore the capitalist system. Stalin's purpose in arranging the trials was to unite the Russian people behind the Communist leadership and provide him with an excuse to keep a tight grip on the country. The main instrument of terror remained the secret police, which changed its name from time to time but never its purpose. Their victims were beaten, tortured, interrogated under bright lights and forced to endure sleeplessness. If this failed, State criminals, as they were called, were subjected to an ever stricter regime that included prolonged solitary confinement or being placed in a punishment cell. Another technique used to gain confessions was to involve the victim's family and it was not surprising that, in the end, many gave in and pleaded guilty to crimes they could not possibly have committed.

The Soviet secret police 1917–43

1917–22 CHEKA	The All Russian Commission to Fight Counter Revolution, Sabotage and Speculation led by Felix Dzerzhinsky
1922–34 OGPU	The Department of Political Police led by Felix Dzerzhinsky and later Genrikh Yagoda. Established as the GPU in 1922, it changed its name to OGPU the following year
1934–43 NKVD	The People's Commissariat of Internal Affairs led in turn by Genrikh Yagoda, Nikolai Yezhov (sometimes spelt Ezhov) and Laventi Beria

The first trials for industrial espionage

In 1928, 53 engineers were arrested in the town of Shakhty in the Donets Basin. It was claimed that they were German agents and were accused of acts of industrial sabotage. They were held responsible for the failure to reach specified production targets. Following their public trial presided over by Andrei Vyshinsky, 11 of the accused were sentenced to death but only five were shot with the remainder being sent to labour camps. Afterwards Stalin commented, 'What do the facts about the Shakhty affair tell us? They tell us that the affair is counter-revolution plotted by some bourgeois specialists…We are dealing with economic intervention by west-European anti-Soviet capitalist organizations…' The case of the Shakhty engineers provided the first trial and executions for economic crimes. In fact, the trial marked the start of a period of terror against specialist workers who were considered unreliable because of their bourgeois backgrounds and the fact that they had acquired their qualifications in tsarist times. With political reliability now considered more important than professional qualifications, waves of arrests of skilled workers followed, all accused of being either enemy agents or Troyskyist sympathizers. Other trials followed and in 1930, some skilled engineers who were members of a 2,000-strong Industrial Party were charged with treason and collaborating with foreign agents. Five were sentenced to death but the sentences were commuted to lengthy terms of imprisonment. The following year, 14 members of the Union Bureau, all former Mensheviks, were charged with trying to interfere in the country's economic development. All pleaded guilty and were sent to prison for between five and ten years. In April 1933, six British engineers employed by the Metropolitan Vickers Electrical Company were arrested by the Russian secret police, the OGPU, and charged with industrial espionage. Even though two confessed, their trial led to a crisis in Anglo-Soviet relations. Some charges levelled against individual workers bordered on the absurd. A Soviet scientist investigating the use of chemicals to destroy weeds was accused of plotting to ruin the nation's harvest whilst a marine biologist was charged with planning to pollute Russian rivers and so destroy the fish stocks!

In the same year, Warsaw-born and St Petersburg University educated Osip Mandelstam wrote a poem about the Russian leader, 'The Stalin Epigram':

We live, deaf to the land beneath us,
Ten steps away no one hears our speeches,

All we hear is the Kremlin mountaineer,
The murderer and peasant-slayer.

His fingers are fat as grubs
And the words, final as lead weights, fall from his lips,

His cockroach whiskers leer
And his boot tops gleam.

Around him a rabble of thin-necked leaders –
Fawning half-men for him to play with.

The whinny, purr or whine
As he prates and points a finger

One by one forging his laws, to be flung
Like horseshoes at the head, to the eye of the groin.

And every killing is a treat
For the broad-chested Ossete*.

> *The term 'Ossete' refers to people who come from
> Azerbaijan and was a reference to a rumour that
> Stalin came from Iranian stock.

Unfortunately for Mandelstam, Stalin did not share his sense of humour. He was arrested and exiled in Cherdyn and, after his release, was re-arrested and sent to a labour camp where he died in 1938. His poem was subsequently described as his '16-line death sentence'. More seriously, in 1934 came the Riutin affair.

The Riutin affair

In 1930, Mikhail Riutin, a one-time member of the Central Committee of the Communist Party and the Party secretary for a district of Moscow, was expelled from the Party for his anti-Stalinist views. He continued to live in Moscow where he worked as an economist. Clearly a courageous if foolhardy man, in 1932 he dared to publish a 200-page document that was highly critical of the Soviet leader. In it, he described Stalin as, 'the evil genius of the Russian revolution who, motivated by personal desire for power and revenge, had brought the revolution to the brink of destruction'. He even went as far as to claim that Stalin had 'broken all records for political hypocrisy and unprincipled political intrigue' and described him as 'the most evil enemy of the Party and the proletarian dictatorship'. He also expressed the view that the proletariat revolution would perish unless Stalin was removed and the entire Party leadership replaced and called for an end to enforced collective farming and a partial return to capitalism. Within the Party and the country as a whole, Riutin was not without supporters!

An outraged Stalin claimed that Riutin and his supporters were out to assassinate him and demanded their arrest and the death penalty for all. However, the Politburo rejected their leader's motion and refused to sanction Riutin's execution. Instead he was sent to a labour camp where he survived until 1937.

Another aspect of the case that troubled Stalin was the fact that many Party members had prior knowledge of Riutin's document and had not reported it. Even worse, several eminent Party members, including Nikolai Bukharin who had earlier been disgraced but then readmitted to the Party, secretly approved of it! Was there really growing opposition to Stalin's rule and, if so, were some members of the Central Committee secretly planning to remove him? In spite of the enthusiasm with which many workers struggled to implement Stalin's economic policies, the harsh working and living conditions imposed upon them led to discontent amongst sections of the proletariat. Within the Party, Riutin was not alone in doubting the wisdom of Stalin's policies and many were also concerned at the increase in exaggerated attempts to win him popularity – the rise of a 'cult of personality' – but was there an obvious challenger for his position? Very popular within the Party was Stalin's close personal friend, the Party leader in Leningrad, Sergei Kirov.

The assassination of Kirov

Today, the name, Kirov is most associated with the famous Leningrad ballet company that was founded in 1935 and took his name. Sergei Kirov, who was originally named Sergei Kostrikov, was born in Urzhum in 1886 and later took the name Kirov as an alias. After the early death of his parents, he was brought up by his grandmother and then at the age of seven, sent to an orphanage. Kirov first showed an interest in Marxism when a student at Kazan Technical School and after moving to Moscow became involved in circulating subversive literature. He was arrested and spent three years in prison. During the civil war, he fought with the Red Army and afterwards became a loyal supporter of Stalin. As a reward, in 1926 he was appointed head of the Communist Party in Leningrad and four years later joined the Politburo. As good looking as he was popular and charismatic, Kirov was regarded as Stalin's protégé and possibly even his eventual successor. Even so, he was quite prepared to challenge his leader and on certain issues gathered enough support to have him outvoted in the Politburo and he particularly infuriated Stalin when he openly called for the rehabilitation of Trotsky and his restoration to the Party. In January 1934, at the Seventeenth Party Congress, the so-called 'Congress of Victors', Kirov chose to stand against Stalin in the election for Party Secretary. Kirov actually won but his success was covered up and the result fixed to allow Stalin, who had held the position since 1923, to continue. In spite of this hiccup in their relationship, Stalin and Kirov continued to holiday together and the Soviet leader urged Kirov to leave Leningrad and join him in Moscow. Was this a sign of their close friendship or did Stalin fear that he was losing control of his protégé and needed to keep a closer eye on him?

On 1 December 1934, Kirov was assassinated at the Communist Party headquarters in Leningrad and a great deal of mystery still surrounds the circumstances of his murder. The assassin, a disillusioned Party member, Leonid Nikolaev, had managed to evade the strict security that normally surrounded Party leaders to carry out the killing. Afterwards, some suggested that Kirov, a well-known womanizer, had been having an affair with his wife. Stalin, who immediately travelled from Moscow to Leningrad to interview Nikolaev, would have none of this and came to a different conclusion. He placed the blame on oppositionists, 'Those comrades who do not confine themselves to criticism and passive resistance but threaten to raise revolt in the Party' and claimed that Trotskyist conspirators had murdered Kirov. In his book, *I Chose Freedom*, Viktor

Kravchenko, a Soviet official who, when posted to Washington, defected to the United States in 1944, recalled:

Stalin and Voroshivov rushed to Leningrad. According to stories circulated in Party circles, Stalin personally supervised the intensive cross-examination. No outsider, of course, could know what he learned, but from his subsequent behaviour it can be surmised that Stalin was alarmed to the point of panic.

Stalin immediately used Kirov's assassination as an excuse to rush through a law, the 'Law of 1 December 1934', which allowed the secret police to speed up the process of arranging the trials and executions of people accused of terrorism and there were to be no appeals allowed against the decisions reached by the courts. Straight away, Genrikh Yagoda, one of the bloodiest of Stalin's secret police chiefs, together with Lev Kamenev and Gregory Zinoviev, who you will remember had earlier supported Trotsky in the power struggle, and 14 other leading members of the Party who had earlier been critical of him, were arrested, subjected to the first great show trial and then executed.

In more recent times, it has been suggested that Stalin himself masterminded Kirov's murder. However, it should be remembered that whilst Kirov had been regarded as a potential replacement for Stalin, he was known as the 'Leningrad dictator' and was himself a hard-line Party man. Alexander Orlov, a former NKVD officer who escaped and sought political asylum in the United States, confirmed that Stalin had arranged the murder of Kirov, 'the beloved son of the Party', as an excuse to begin the liquidation of unreliable Politburo members. Later, in 1956, at the Twentieth Congress of the Soviet Communist Party and three years after Stalin's death, Nikita Khrushchev came close to repeating these accusations when he said 'many prominent Party leaders and rank-and-file Party workers, honest and dedicated to the cause of communism, fell victim to Stalin's despotism…he was guilty of the most cruel oppression, violating all norms of revolutionary legality by acting against anyone who in any way disagreed with him'.

However, the case against Stalin is far from proven with certainty. It can be claimed that Kirov was himself a hard-line Communist who did not really offer a radical alternative to Stalin. Perhaps more sinister was the possible involvement of the secret police, the NKVD, now led by Laventy Beria. It appears that they had previously arrested and then released the assassin, Nikolaev, and then failed to adequately protect Kirov. Strangely too, Kirov's personal bodyguard, Borisov, the only man to actually witness the assassination, died in a road accident the following day whilst travelling with a group of KGB agents. It was later claimed that he was thrown from the car. During his cross-examination, Nikolaev insisted that he had no contacts with any opposition groups and had acted alone but his evidence, that was confused and contradictory, did not prevent him being executed together with 13 other alleged accomplices. In addition, a further 103 people with no apparent connection with the crime were also shot – and this was only the beginning!

In her *20 Letters to a Friend*, Stalin's daughter, Svetlana Allilueva, who was firmly convinced of her father's innocence, wrote:

> *Kirov used to live in our house. He was one of us, an old colleague and friend... He was closer to us than any of his colleagues and my father needed him. I would never believe that my father was involved in his death. It would be more logical to link his killing with the name of Beria.*

However, guilty or not, the murder of Kirov certainly provided Stalin with the excuse to tighten his grip on the people and triggered a series of massive purges and show trials that led to the deaths of thousands, perhaps even millions, of people, a great many of them innocent of the charges made against them.

Purges and show trials

As we have seen, the first major show trial followed quickly after Kirov's murder. The most prominent victims were the so-called Old Bolsheviks, those who had been eminent Party members during the events of 1917 and the civil war that followed. Some, such as Lev Kamenev and Grigory Zinoviev, had earlier been supporters of Trotsky and both had been expelled from the Party. After making their peace with Stalin, they had been allowed to return but now the Russian leader turned on them once again and accused both men of being in league with the exiled Trotsky, playing a part in the murder of Kirov and stirring up discontent. Their prosecution was left to the notorious Andrei Vyshinsky.

Earlier Vyshinsky, a Ukrainian born in Odessa in 1883, had sided with the Mensheviks and did not become a member of the Communist Party until 1920. A qualified lawyer and university lecturer, he turned his skills to specializing as a prosecuting attorney and it was he who had earlier successfully prosecuted those accused of industrial espionage. As a prosecutor, he earned the reputation of being aggressive, vengeful and cunning and he willingly accepted uncorroborated evidence and confessions obtained by torture. He was to play a major role in the purge trials that lay ahead.

At the trial of Kamenev and Zinoviev, Vyshinsky tried to get the accused men to implicate others such as Lenin's favourite and the former rising star of the Party, Aleksei Rykov, the trade union leader, Mikhail Tomsky and the sophisticated and scholarly Nicolai Bukharin who had supported Stalin and agreed with his view of trying to achieve 'socialism in one country'. The three men were arrested and investigated but all refused to confess to the ludicrous charges made against them and their trials had to be called off...at least for the time being. Later and in accordance with Stalin's wishes, Kamenev and Zinoviev were re-arrested and Vyshinsky found both guilty and ordered them to be shot.

Genrikh Yagoda, head of the secret police, was to pay for his failure to get confessions and was replaced by Nikolai Yezhov. Nicknamed the 'bloody dwarf' because of his cruelty and lack of stature, Yezhov was to give his name to the most bloody period of the purges, the 'Yezhovshchina' or 'evil times of Yezhov'. Some allege that Yezhov's reputation for sadism was due in part to his dependence on drugs and his entry in the current *Who's Who in Russia and the Former USSR* describes him as 'one of the most repulsive figures of the Stalin era'.

The second major show trial began in January 1937. This time the leading accused included Grigorii Pyatokov, who was supposedly responsible for a series of explosions in some Siberian mines, Karl Radek, a specialist in international affairs who had formerly supported Trotsky, and Commissar of Finance, Grigorii Sokolnikov, who had been one of the signatories of the Treaty of Brest-Litovsk. This time Vyshinsky really went to town describing them not only as Trotskyites but also 'vipers, liars, clowns and insignificant pigmies'. All pleaded guilty and pleaded for their lives to be spared, while Radek and Sokolnikov were sentenced to ten years imprisonment, the remainder were shot. The Communist authorities tried to convince the Russian people that the events taking place were in their interest but although many didn't see it that way, they wisely chose to remain silent.

Stalin next purged the armed services of its leaders. The most famous soldier to stand trial was Marshal Mikhail Tukhachevsky. Born into a noble family of Polish origin, he had served as an officer in the tsarist army until 1918 when he joined the Bolsheviks for reasons of career advancement rather than political conviction. One of the founders of the Red Army and a leading military strategist, he had fought with distinction in the civil war and in 1921 played a leading part in crushing the Kronstadt mutiny. By far the best-known senior officer in the Red Army, he was very popular and in 1935 became a Marshal of the Soviet Union. Ironically, he had earlier travelled to London to represent the Russian government at the funeral of King George V and was scheduled to attend the coronation of King George VI! Accused of being part of a 'gigantic conspiracy' and plotting with foreign powers, Tukhachevsky and several other leading generals and admirals were found guilty and shot. Determined to take over total control of the armed forces, Stalin next authorized the arrest of over 35,000 serving officers. When all was settled, only two generals out of five and less than half of the junior officers remained so that in a matter of months, the leadership of the Red Army and Navy was decimated.

In the meantime, Yezhov and Vyshinsky ensured that the terror continued unabated. In 1937, the Politburo legalized the use of torture during the inquisition of prisoners and Yezhov set targets of those to be arrested and shot in each district.

The last of the great show trials began in Moscow in March 1938. Now time had run out for Nicolai Bukharin, Andrei Rykov and the former head of the secret police, Genrikh Yagoda. Mikhail Tomsky would have certainly been included had he not committed suicide beforehand. In presenting the case against the accused, Vyshinsky's imagination reached new realms of fantasy as he claimed that in 1918 they had all been part of a plot to murder Lenin and more recently they had been involved in a conspiracy with German and Japanese agents to partition the Soviet Union and then restore capitalism. Screaming and ranting, Vyshinsky described them as not merely being a band of 'felonious criminals' but also of being 'the basest, lowest, and most contemptible, the most depraved of the depraved'. He continued:

The whole country is demanding one thing. The traitors and spies who were selling our country must be shot like dirty dogs. Our people are demanding one thing. Crush the accursed reptile. Time will pass and the graves of the hateful traitors will grow over with weeds and thistles. But over us, over our happy country, our sun will shine... Over the road cleared of the last scum and filth of the past, we, with our beloved leader and teacher, the great Stalin, at our head, we will march as before onwards and onwards towards Communism.

It was a powerful condemnation but Bukharin was not a man easily cowed and standing before the court he made one last statement:

> *I am perhaps speaking for the last time in my life...I am kneeling before the country, before the Party, before the whole people...As I await the verdict...what matters is not the personal feelings of a repentant enemy, but the flourishing progress of the USSR.*

After being condemned to death, Andrei Rykov wrote a letter to the Supreme Soviet asking for clemency:

> *I ask you to believe that I am not a completely corrupt person. In my life there were many years of noble, honest work for the Revolution. I can still prove that even after committing so many crimes, it is possible to become an honest person and to die with honour. I ask that you spare my life.*

Since the sentences had been decided beforehand, it was to no avail and both men were duly shot.

Foreign observers who attended the show trials were astounded that so many obviously innocent people, many of them Old Bolsheviks who had been prominent in the events of 1917 and were still dedicated Communists, pleaded guilty to crimes they could not have possibly committed. Quite incredibly, some pleaded guilty because they earnestly believed that their sacrifice was in the interests of the Soviet people but others who stood in the dock appeared to be bewildered and disorientated. The truth was that before being sent for trial, they had been held in the cellars of the secret police headquarters in Lubyanka prison and subject to threats, torture and sometimes even drugged. It was said that anyone tortured by the NKVD would never again be able to walk or stand upright and would be mentally scarred for life. The few who could not be broken were not sent for trial but were executed in their cells by a shot in the back of the head.

The Moscow show trials were but the tip of the iceberg. Across the Soviet Union, tens of thousands of people were purged and eliminated. The situation threatened to get out of hand as Party members competed to denounce each other and, so they claimed, cleanse the Party of those who were half-hearted or unreliable. In truth, they were attempting to show their loyalty to Stalin's regime and so save their own skins. Such treachery was often used as a means of acquiring promotion to a Party member's position, or his property or even his wife and in some instances, as a way of settling old scores. By the end of 1938, the Russian Communist Party had lost a third of its members. The American writer Frank Smith described the mass hysteria of the time:

> *In factories and offices mass meetings were held in which people were urged to be vigilant against sabotage. It was up to them to make the distinction between incompetence and intentional wrecking and any mishap might be blamed on wrecking. Denunciations were common. Neighbours denounced neighbours. Denunciations were a good way of striking against people one did not like, including one's parents, a way of eliminating people blocking one's promotion...and a means of proving one's patriotism. Many realized that some innocent people were being victimized and the saying went around that*
> *When you chop wood, the chips fly.*

One of those best able to describe ridiculous reasons for denunciation and the suffering of those sent to the Gulags was Aleksandr Solzhenitsyn, who in the latter years of Stalin's rule spent time in a corrective labour camp. In his book, *The Gulag Archipelago*, he tells of a tailor who accidentally stuck a needle in a picture of a member of the Politburo and, accused of an act of terrorism, was sent to a labour camp for ten years. A woman who allowed a bar of soap to fall on a picture of the head of Stalin whilst shopping was also sentenced to ten years! The vast complex of prison camps that stretched from the desolate regions close to the Finnish border and then across the icy wastes of inhospitable Siberian Russia contained thousands of men and women intended for use as slave labour. The conditions they had to tolerate and the demands placed upon them meant that ten years in such camps usually meant death. A prisoner recalled:

> *They didn't show thermometers to the workers, it wasn't necessary – they had to go out to work in any temperature. Anyway old hands could determine the degree of frost exactly without a thermometer; if there is a frosty fog, that means that outside it is minus 40 degrees centigrade; if breathing upon exhaling goes out with a noise, but it's still not hard to breath, that means minus 45 degrees; if breathing is noisy and there's a noticeable shortage of breath, minus 50 degrees. Below minus 50 degrees, spit freezes.*
>
> From *Kolyma Tales* by Varlam Shalamov, 1966

Figure 7.1 *The location of the labour camps (Gulags) across the Soviet Union.*

Relatives of those accused and arrested, including wives and children as young as 12, became obvious suspects and were liable to arrest. Wives usually lost their jobs and means of support and either had to sell their possessions or themselves in order to survive. In fact, women accounted for only a relatively small number of those sentenced to long prison terms. Overall then, just how many were arrested, convicted and executed by the secret police?

Table 7.1   *Arrests, convictions and executions by the NKVD 1934–8*

	Arrests (all crimes)	*Arrests (counter-revolutionary crimes)*	*Convictions*	*Executions*
1934	205,173	90,417	78,999	2,056
1935	193,083	108,935	267,076	1,229
1936	131,168	91,127	274,670	1,118
1937	936,750	779,056	790,665	353,074
1938	638,509	593,326	554,258	328,618

Source: GARF (from a report prepared by Stalin's successors after 1953)

There have been various estimates about the number of people who died in the death camps of the 'Gulag archipelago'. In *The Great Terror: Stalin's Purge of the Thirties*, Robert Conquest suggests 9 million but the estimates of other historians vary between 12 and 24 million. The chances are that because of the absence of accurate records and the number of victims shot out of hand by the secret police went unrecorded, the true number will never be known.

By early 1939, Yezhov, who was to eventually suffer the same fate as his victims, was replaced by Beria as head of the NKVD and the worst of the mass arrests and trials came to an end. Many were released from the labour camps and many restored their membership of the Party. At the Communist Party Congress held in March 1939, Stalin seemed unrepentant when he told the assembled delegates:

> It cannot be said that the cleansings were not accompanied by grave mistakes. There were unfortunately more mistakes than might have been expected. Undoubtedly, we shall have no further need to resort to the method of mass cleansings. Nevertheless, the cleansings of 1933–6 were unavoidable and their results, on the whole, were beneficial.

The 'Terror' – an overview

Even after the passing of time, several aspects of the Stalinist purges are still the subject of debate amongst historians and many questions remain unanswered Firstly, why did Stalin plunge his country into a state of terror and send millions of Party members and ordinary individuals to their deaths by summary execution or overwork and starvation in the atrocious conditions in the gulags? Was it simply the case that a man consumed by paranoia and a callous disregard for human life ruled the Soviet Union?

The view most commonly held is that Stalin had a lust for power and that the Terror was a tool he used deliberately to destroy his rivals and those opposed to his policies and, at the same time, indicate to the Russian people that he would not tolerate any opposition to his rule. He was certainly taken aback by the fact that, in 1934, Michail Riutin's criticisms of his policies had found so much support amongst members of the Central Committee and the fact that Sergei Kirov had the nerve to stand against him in the election of Party Secretary. He was also aware of rivalries and policy differences within the Party and that beyond Moscow, regional Party leaders often went their own way and failed to follow the official line. However, Stalin's real concern was with the questionable loyalty of Old Bolsheviks such as Bukharin, Kamenev, Radek, Rykov and Zinoviev, the men who had been involved in the events of 1917 and the civil war that followed and whose original loyalties had been to Lenin. Then was there the possibility that military leaders such as Tukhachevsky might be planning a coup against him? Such men had once served in Trotsky's Red Army and many still showed great affection for their former leader.

Again, was Stalin's Terror merely a continuation the terror inaugurated by Lenin at the time of the revolution and the civil war? Was it possible that Stalin was merely out to protect his Communist state from the threat of counter-revolution? Was it even possible that Stalin was a deranged psychopath? In her book *Stalin: Man of Steel*, Elizabeth Roberts comments, 'It is doubtful if a truly sane man would have done as Stalin did'.

If Stalin was the man behind the purges, was he solely responsible or were others involved? Surely brutal and vindictive as he was, he must have had accomplices. The most obvious were the heads of the NKVD, Genrikh Yagoda and Nikolai Yezhov, and there is some justice in the fact that both were themselves to become victims of the purges. In 1937, Yagoda was charged with treason and murder and two years later, Yezhov was found guilty of treason and both were shot. Andrei Vyshinsky, Stalin's obedient and merciless prosecutor, also played a leading role in the purge trials. Described by Leonard Schapiro as 'the nearest thing to a rat that I have ever seen', Vyshinsky showed great skill in retaining the confidence of his leader. In 1940, he was appointed a Deputy Commissar for Foreign Affairs and, in 1949, became Soviet Foreign Minister. In addition, behind the scenes there must have been thousands of Party officials and NKVD officers who made life and death decisions and willingly took part in the killings. Some enjoyed the exercise of power and being able to inflict suffering on others.

The impact and repercussions of the purges and show trials

An obvious repercussion of the purges and show trials was their impact on public opinion both at home and abroad. Whilst ordinary Russians dared not register their disapproval of what was happening, the foreign press enjoyed a field day with lurid accounts of trials and executions. From his place of exile in Mexico, Trotsky commented sarcastically about the Soviet leader, 'I am right in saying I have never rated Stalin so highly as to be able to hate him.' Of the trials, he wrote:

> *How could these old Bolsheviks who went through the jails and exiles of tsarism, who were heroes of the civil war, the leaders of industry, the builders of the Party...turn out to be saboteurs, allies of fascism, organizers of espionage, agents of capitalist restoration? Who can believe such accusations? How can anyone be made to believe them? And why is Stalin compelled to tie up in the fate of his personal rule with these monstrous, impossible, nightmarish judicial trials?*

Many of those murdered or sent to the camps were many of the Party bureaucrats. They were usually replaced by younger men who were known to be more dedicated to Stalin but lacked the experience of their predecessors. This led to administrative disruption at both national and local levels. The removal of suspect teachers and lecturers had an adverse effect on the education system whilst industry suffered because of the loss of many of its best managers and engineers. Those who replaced them were often poorly trained and not suitably skilled. The removal of so many senior military men and the near elimination of the officer class left the armed services lacking experienced leadership and this at a time when German aggression was threatening to plunge Europe into war.

A final score to settle – the murder of Leon Trotsky

You will recall that from their very first meeting, Stalin took a dislike to Trotsky that turned into a deep-seated hatred. This increased further when the two men became embroiled in a leadership contest during which Stalin outwitted and outmanoeuvred his rival. There is little doubt that if Trotsky had called upon the army to support him, he might have been able to seize power but instead he appeared to relinquish his powers both easily and readily. The explanation is that Trotsky's first loyalty was to the Communist Party and it would have been unthinkable for him to use the army against the Party. However noble his intentions, by the time he realized his error of judgement, it was too late. Stalin saw to it that he was removed from his position as head of the army and instead he was given a minor role and placed in charge of a programme of electrification. Later, expelled from the Party and finally sent into exile, Trotsky travelled in turn to Turkey, France and Norway before settling in Mexico. In 1929, he applied for a British visa but this was refused although at the time the playwright Bernard Shaw advised those who 'had an unreasoned dread of him as a caged lion' to allow him into the country 'if only to hold the key to his cage'! In the end, Mexico was the only country prepared to grant him political asylum. He became something of a popular celebrity there and attracted a great deal of attention from his place of exile as he wrote books and newspaper articles and gave well attended lectures. He took every opportunity to pour scorn on Stalin and denounced the Communist system that he had imposed on the Russian people. Aware that one of the charges invariably levelled against those arrested during the purges was that they were Trotskyists, he described the show trials as 'the greatest frame-up in history' and claimed that Stalin had ignored the interests of the proletariat in order to secure his own position and promote his own self-interest. In Moscow an enraged Stalin bided his time as he waited for the chance to silence his critic. In 1938, Trotsky's son, Leon Sedov, was murdered whilst receiving hospital treatment in Paris and shortly afterwards the headless body of one of his closest friends was found floating in the River Seine. Well aware that he was a likely target of NKVD assassins, Trotsky took steps to turn his home, where he lived with his wife, Natala, and their family, in Coyoacan on the outskirts of Mexico City, into a fortress. Living behind high stone walls and windows with steel shutters, he employed security guards to keep a close check on all visitors. Meanwhile he continued to write books, give interviews and care for his pet rabbits. In May 1940, Trotsky escaped unharmed when men used a house facing his home to spray his bedroom with bullets. Later that year, a seemingly trustworthy man, Ramon Mercador, managed to win

Trotsky's confidence by pretending to be sympathetic in his politics. A handsome and sophisticated man of Spanish origin, he used several aliases and seduced the sister of the revolutionary's secretary. On 20 August, being well known to the guards, Mercador easily gained admittance to the house, went to Trotsky's study and plunged an ice axe into his head as he sat at his desk. In spite of efforts to save his life, he fell into a coma and died the following day at the age of 61.

At his trial, Mercador was sentenced to 20 years' imprisonment, whilst in Moscow his mother received the Honour of Lenin on his behalf from Stalin. In his testament written shortly before his death, Trotsky wrote –

> *I have no need here to once gain refute the stupid and vile slanders of Stalin...I have never entered, directly or indirectly, into any behind the scenes agreements with the enemies of the working class...*
>
> *For 43 years of my conscious life I have remained a revolutionist; for 42 of them I have fought under the banner of Marxism. If I had to begin all over again, I would of course try to avoid this and that mistake, but the main course of my life would remain unchanged. I shall die a proletarian revolutionist, a Marxist, a dialectical materialist* and consequently, an irreconcilable atheist. My faith in the communist future of mankind is not less ardent, indeed it is firmer today than it was in the days of my youth.*
>
> *Natasha has just come up to the window from the courtyard and opened it wider so that the air may enter more freely into my room. I can see the bright green strip of grass beneath the wall, and the clear blue sky above the wall, and sunlight everywhere. Life is beautiful. Let the future generations cleanse it of all evil, oppression and violence and enjoy it to the full.'*
>
> From *Trotsky, a documentary* by Francis Wyndham and David King, 1972

*Dialectical materialism was Karl Marx's view of history as a conflict between opposing forces representing the interests of capitalists and workers that would eventually lead to a class struggle.

So it was finally over. The assassination of Trotsky completed Stalin's systematic and bloody terror aimed against a generation of Old Bolsheviks. When Mercador was released from prison in 1960, he left Mexico for Cuba and then Prague before travelling to Moscow.

8

....

Everyday life in Stalin's Russia

This chapter will cover:
- *marriage, children and the family*
- *living conditions*
- *the Soviet education system*
- *the youth movement, Komsomol*
- *the role of women in Soviet society*
- *Stalin's family.*

  Life has become better. Life has become merrier.

From a speech made by Stalin in 1936

The family

You will remember that after the October Revolution, Lenin's Bolsheviks declared marriage a bourgeois institution that gave men the opportunity to exploit women. They also issued numerous decrees that relaxed the laws relating to marriage, children and divorce and these were included in a marriage law book, the aim of which was to break the hold of the Russian Orthodox Church on the people. Some Communists went as far as to claim that children were better brought up in State-run homes rather than by their parents at home! Divorce became easy since to dissolve a marriage, one partner only had to make a simple declaration at a registry office without even informing the other. This led to promiscuity, a breakdown in family life with an increase in crime, sexual permissiveness and the abortion rate, and inner cities were plagued by bands of orphaned or abandoned children who begged or stole in order to survive. In 1927, Stalin, who had disagreed with the permissive measures, stated

'The state cannot exist without the family' and took steps to revise the law in an attempt to restore traditional attitudes and ensure that the family unit formed the basis of the Soviet society. The State granted an allowance of 2,000 roubles a year to mothers who had six or more children. As we have seen, he made divorce more difficult, restricted contraception, banned abortion and increased the penalties for criminal behaviour. Similarly, homosexuality, tolerated in the 1920s, became an offence in 1934 with offenders liable to five years imprisonment.

Living conditions

In urban areas, overcrowding was a major problem and it was not unusual to find several generations of the same family living together in a one-room apartment in one of the new high-rise blocks. In Moscow, only 6 per cent of the apartments consisted of more than one room! Those with no housing often slept on the stairways and in corridors. Grandparents, parents and their children would live, eat and sleep in the most cramped conditions and share communal kitchens, washrooms and toilets with families in other apartments. Pots, pans and all cooking utensils were communal. Although electricity was available, it was often in short supply, as was running water. The housing blocks, speedily constructed and shoddy by Western standards, were state owned and consequently little effort was made to keep them in a good state of repair. Broken windows were boarded up and the space around window frames stuffed with paper and rags to keep out the cold. It was not surprising that infestation with vermin led to the spread of infectious diseases and since kerosene needed for heating was difficult to come by, the cold and damp conditions led to acute rheumatic conditions. Of course, the living conditions described above did not apply to the new breed of State officials and bureaucrats who not only enjoyed better housing but were able to employ servants and entertain.

Even though it had been promised, the collectivization of agriculture did not immediately create an abundance of food. You will recall that Stalin believed that food was a reward for hard work and those unable to work received severely reduced rations. Bread was dark and heavy and contained thick, unground grains. Meat and fish, dairy produce, salt and sugar were also scarce and when they did appear had to be queued for. In fact, queuing became a way of life with women beginning to form queues in freezing temperatures early in the morning and then moving from one queue to another. Only too often they found the stock exhausted by the time they reached the head of the queue. The situation was eased by the fact that most workers had at least one meal a day at their work's canteen, which meant that their rations could be used for providing meals at home. There was little point in complaining since this risked having one's rations reduced and, anyway, something was better than nothing. Officially food rationing ended in 1935 but in reality this only led to greater shortages and even longer queues.

Clothing was also scarce, drab and uniform-like and extremely badly made by unskilled workers employed in the textile industry. Most clothing had to be frequently altered and repaired whilst children depended on hand-me-downs. The loss of livestock at the start of the programme of collectivization meant that leather became scarce and so, consequently, did footwear.

Living conditions in the countryside were little better. Whilst peasants may not have suffered the acute overcrowding of urban workers and food may have been a little more abundant, there was usually no electricity, running water or adequate sanitation available. In both town and country there was a flourishing black market in food and clothing but those found guilty of illicit trading were treated like criminals and sentenced to terms of imprisonment.

Although health care had been greatly expanded and there were more doctors than ever before, the fact that treatment was free led to a heavy demand and the expected qualified medical help was often unavailable when needed. Gradually an increasing number of sports clubs and stadia were provided by the State and this helped to improve fitness standards and arouse interest in sport. The most popular sports that attracted large crowds of spectators were football, athletics, gymnastics and ice hockey. Chess players, particularly the grandmasters, were also held in high esteem. Every Russian was entitled to a holiday each year but accommodation at State-run hotels and resorts was limited.

Homelessness was also a problem. As men left the collective farms to try to find work in the industrial areas, so there was always a goodly number who could find no accommodation and were forced to sleep rough and survive by scrounging or theft. The deportation of the kulaks and the years of starvation meant that thousands of abandoned and orphaned children were left to fend for themselves. As State orphanages struggled to cope, so street gangs contributed to the country's soaring crime rate. A law passed in 1938 imposed harsh penalties on young offenders with the death penalty being applied to children over the age of 12. Parents were also held responsible for the behaviour of their troublesome children and if they were sent to penal institutions, they had to pay for their upkeep.

Education

THE BOLSHEVIK VIEW

During the years following the Revolution, the Bolsheviks appeared to be disinterested in learning since they regarded the educational needs of the proletariat to be only minimal. They were of the opinion that the only education required could best be achieved through a system of learning known as 'productive labour' and in Moscow, the head of the Institute for Educational Research stated that the *method proektov*, the project method, was the one and only truly Marxist method of teaching. This method involved sending children into factories to learn skills by gaining experience working alongside the workers. Some Marxist theorists were even of the opinion that the need for education would gradually 'wither away'. Young children were taught by *babushkas* (the name *babushka* comes from the triangular headscarf worn by old women), old women who cared for children at home, or by their grandmothers and the responsibility for providing schools was passed to the managers of the collective farms and industrial enterprises. The schools that came into existence abandoned traditional teaching methods and only provided the most elementary instruction often by adults who were themselves barely literate. Where schools existed, places were allocated on a quota system based on social class. The children of the proletariat were the most favoured whilst those of the former bourgeoisie were assigned few places or none at all. At that time, Russia's few universities provided tuition in a limited range of practical subjects taught to a dismally low level. The problem was that former university lecturers were considered relics of the now discredited academic bourgeoisie and, baited and humiliated, were driven out of the profession. With examinations scrapped, the level of achievement was poor and with a high drop-out rate, three-quarters of all students failed to complete their courses!

THE STALINIST VIEW

Under Stalin's dictatorship, the Soviet education system changed radically. Out went the *method proektov* and with the need for a sound education now recognized, plans were made to implement a programme intended to extend nursery, primary, secondary and further education across the country. Experimentation came to an end and traditional teaching methods were restored together with strict classroom discipline and the requirement to wear school uniform whilst girls had to style their hair in plaits. The new system provided nursery schools for children under the age of three followed by four years in an infant school or kindergarten. Children then transferred to secondary schools where attendance was compulsory until the age of 15 and parents were expected to make some financial contribution towards their children's education during the final years at school.

A common core of subjects was taught with special emphasis placed on the need for obedience, hard work and loyalty. Pupils were also subject to a degree of political indoctrination. With over 100 different languages taught across the breadth of the Soviet Union, pupils were allowed to study in their own native tongue but learning Russian was made compulsory for all. A system of examinations was reintroduced which was rigorous and every pupil was expected to have gained some success by the time they left school.

Whilst policy decisions were made by the Central Committee of the Communist Party, the overall responsibility for the provision of education now lay with *Narkompros*, the People's Commissariat for Enlightenment. The Commissariat kept tight control over such matters as curricula and textbooks. Each of the republics of the Soviet Union had its own education ministry and in each locality members of the local Soviet appointed a school board. The boards selected the headteachers who in turn appointed their own teaching staff. Advancement within the teaching profession usually depended on one's standing in the Party. Two prominent educationalists of the time were Anatoly Lunarcharsky and Alexander Bubnov. Lunarcharsky, a charismatic, well-educated and cultured man, was a dedicated Communist and, known as the 'Poet of the Revolution', he was largely responsible for turning many of the country's stately homes into museums. Bubnov, a staunch supporter of Stalin's educational reforms, was responsible for ending the period of experiment and returning to traditional teaching methods. With the status of teachers and lecturers restored, more young people were encouraged to enter further education. *Rabfak*, the Workers' Faculty, was set up to provide educational opportunities for working men and women and many tried to improve themselves by joining adult education classes. Amongst those to benefit from this provision were Nikita Khrushchev, a future Soviet leader, and the aircraft designer, Sergei Ilyushin. In 1931, Stalin called for the creation of a new Soviet intelligentsia:

> **No ruling class has managed without its own intelligentsia. There are grounds for believing that the working class of the USSR can manage without its own industrial and technical intelligentsia. The Soviet Government has taken this circumstance into account and has opened wide the doors of all higher educational institutions in every branch of the national economy to members of the working class and labouring peasantry.**

Entry to higher education was by competitive examination and with the restriction on students from bourgeois backgrounds removed, there was no shortage of young people seeking admission. To begin with, a fixed percentage of places in higher education were allocated to women but this soon became unnecessary since by 1940, 60 per cent of all undergraduates were women. From a racial viewpoint, 80 per cent of all students were ethnic Russians, Ukrainians and Jews with relatively few coming from the country's Asian republics. At universities and technical colleges, a special emphasis was placed on the study of mathematics, science and technology and preparation to play a part in the life of a modern industrial state. As citizens of a Communist state, they were expected to be hard working, to show an appreciation of Party ideology by spurning capitalism, to show patriotism in the form of love for Mother Russia and to reject religion. By 1936 the country's system of higher education was producing large numbers of well-trained engineers, scientists, doctors, lecturers and teachers – all, as Stalin put it, examples of 'the new Soviet man'.

Soviet youth movements

Away from schools and educational institutions, the Soviet regime tried to indoctrinate its young people by encouraging them to enroll in Communist youth organizations. The twin aims of membership were to instill in the young an appreciation of Communist ideology and prepare them for their role as the next generation of Communists. For the very young, there was the Little Octobrists and at the age of nine, they transferred to the *Vsesoyuzny Leninsky Communistichesky*, All Union Lenin Pioneer Organization. Divided into brigades, it ran politically orientated educational and recreational activities. On enrollment, a Pioneer had to make a pledge:

> *I, a Young Pioneer of the Soviet Union, solemnly promise in the presence of my comrades*
>
> ▶ *to warmly love my Soviet motherland*
>
> ▶ *to live, study and to struggle as Lenin willed and as the Communist Party teaches.*

At the age of 14, they became eligible to join the *Kommunisticheski Soyuz Molodezhi*, abbreviated to Komsomol. Membership of Komsomol included young people aged between 14 and 28 and the movement first came into being during the civil war when units of young men were recruited to fight alongside the Red Army. At that time, it had over 400,000 members. After 1922, it reverted to its role as a youth movement and offered its members the opportunity to join in educational and sporting activities and become engaged in industrial projects. During the Five-Year Plans, the movement provided thousands of volunteers to work on major projects in the Dombass region and at Magnitogorsk and also contributed to the building of the Moscow metro. Numerous advantages could be gained through membership of Komsomol such as being favoured in matters of employment and promotion and the possible award of scholarships. More important, membership of Komsomol helped when applying for the much coveted membership of the Communist Party.

The role of women in the Soviet Union

In tsarist Russia, the feminist movement was virtually non-existent and with only limited legal rights, women were subordinate to men. Marx was of the opinion that marriage was a bourgeois institution that contributed to the exploitation and oppression of women. He said:

> *Women in the (capitalist) system became instruments of production, reproduction and gratification. Love, like all other human virtues, has been turned into a marketable commodity and capitalist society thus has become a giant whorehouse.*

Lenin agreed and wrote complaining of:

> *...the calm acquiescence of men who see how women grow worn out in petty, monstrous household work; their strength and time dissipated and wasted, their minds growing stale and narrow, their hearts beating slowly, their wills weakened.*

Once in power the Bolsheviks granted women full citizenship and equality in economic, political and family life. They also introduced a Marxist-based Family Code that made marriage a civil ceremony and allowed easier divorce. Consequently, by the mid-1920s the Soviet Union had the highest divorce rate in Europe, in some areas the number of abortions exceeded the number of live births and nationally there was an alarming fall in the birth rate. As we have seen, Stalin's new Code on Marriage, Family and Guardianship of 1927 reversed the situation. In 1922, women made up just a quarter of the industrial labour force but, Stalin's Five-Year Plans made the mass entry of women into the workplace necessary so that by 1940 this had increased to just under 40 per cent. Although, in theory, the Russian Constitution guaranteed female workers equality with their male counterparts, in practice, discrimination continued. In addition, the fact that a woman was employed in factory work on a full-time basis did not diminish her domestic responsibilities as a housewife and a mother – housework and the care of the children. Child bearing did not absolve mothers from their commitment to work and granted only minimum maternity leave, young children had to be left in the care of elderly relatives and friends and there were instances when mothers had to suffer the indignity of transferring milk from their breasts to bottles so that the feeding of their infants did not interrupt their work routine. Still Party propaganda continued to emphasize that the ideal woman should be a good wife and mother as well as a good worker.

Zhenotdel

In the Soviet Union, policy decisions relating to women were placed in the hands of the women's section of the Central Committee, the *Zhenotdel*, the Women's Bureau. Originally set up to encourage women to play a more active part in the political and economic life of the country, the leaders of *Zhenotdel* were the eminent Party members and feminists, Aleksandra Kollontai and Inessa Armand who both came from bourgeois family backgrounds. Kollontai was the daughter of a general and although married to an officer in the tsarist army, she had become an active revolutionary and was forced to live in exile in the United States. After returning to Russia in 1917, Lenin appointed her commissar for social welfare. Kollontai later joined the diplomatic service and was the first woman to hold ambassadorial rank. Twice married and the mother of five children, Armand was a close friend of Lenin and became the first director of *Zhenotdel*. Representatives of the Bureau toured factories to ensure that the legislation intended to protect the rights of women was being correctly enforced. Convinced that education provided women with a better chance of improving their status, *Zhenotdel* organized childcare facilities that would allow them to study in their spare time.

The activities of *Zhenotdel* did not receive universal approval. From the start, many men, including senior Party officials and even groups of women workers, opposed their policies whilst in the Soviet Union's Islamic republics, Muslims resented their attempts to abolish polygamy and the traditional seclusion of women, purdah. The Bureau also failed in its attempt to enroll women as Communist Party members with less than 15 per cent of women applying for membership, no female representation on the country's ruling Presidium and very few on the influential Central Committee. In 1930, claiming to have achieved its aims, *Zhenotdel* was closed down.

In 1937, Stalin, seemingly oblivious to the realities of the situation, wrote:

> *The triumph of socialism has filled women with enthusiasm and mobilized the women of our Soviet land to become active in culture, to master machinery, to develop a knowledge of science and to be active in the struggle for high labour productivity.*

During the period 1928–40, the number of working women in the Soviet Union rose from 3 to 13 million and whilst a great many worked shoulder to shoulder with their male counterparts in factories, some were employed in steel works and coalmines where they were encouraged to become *stakhanovi* – female Stakhanovites. At the same time an increasing number of women was employed in what were to become female-dominated occupations – office work, nursing and teaching – whilst at the other end of the scale, some worked in far more menial jobs such as street cleaning and refuse removal. An even greater demand was to be made on women during the Second World War when the best part of a million were recruited for the armed forces with many of them serving as combat soldiers.

...and what of Stalin and his own family?

You will recall that in 1905, the young Josef Stalin had married Ekaterina Svanidze. A son, Yakov, was born to them in 1908 but the following year, Ekaterina died. Eleven years later, 39-year-old Stalin married for a second time and this time his bride was the 16-year-old daughter of an old Georgian revolutionary friend, Nadezhda Alliluyeva. They were to have two children, Vasili, born in 1921, and a daughter, Svetlana, in 1926. There marriage grew increasingly tempestuous and there were frequent rows. Nadezhda disliked her husband's cult of personality and she was given to openly questioning his policies. This led to a stormy relationship with frequent quarrels, deterioration in her mental state and depression. On 9 November 1932, she was found dead in her bedroom with a revolver by her side. At the time, it was said to be suicide but rumours persist that she was killed on Stalin's orders or even by his own hand. There is also the view that his wife's death unhinged him and sent him on a course of mass terror. As we shall see, Stalin's children and their families were to suffer at his hands in much the same way as any other.

It is also claimed that in 1908, Stalin had an illegitimate son, Constantin, a consequence of his relationship with a young widow, Maria Kuzakova. In 1995, Constantin Kuzakov wrote an exposé of this in his book, *Kuzakoz: Son of Stalin.*

9

Soviet foreign policy, 1918–40

This chapter will cover:
- *attitudes to Russia after the Revolution*
- *the Communist International – Comintern*
- *Stalin's diplomacy during the 1920s*
- *the Anti-Comintern Pact and Stalin's search for collective security*
- *Russian involvement in the Spanish Civil War*
- *the Soviet attitude to the Czech crisis of 1938*
- *the Ribbentrop-Molotov Pact, 1939*
- *the 'Winter War' against Finland.*

> *Stalin did appear to have an underlying motive (in foreign policy):*
> *to provide external security for the internal construction of*
> *communism.*
>
> *Stalin and the Soviet Union* by Stephen J. Lee, 1999

Soviet foreign policy in the 1920s

It may appear strange that at the start Soviet foreign policy after
the Revolution of 1918 differed very little from that of former
tsarist times. Both the tsars and the Bolsheviks sought to protect
Russia from outside influences and both wanted to extend Russian
influence in the Middle and Far East. Of course, Lenin had enough
on his plate in consolidating Bolshevik rule and what foreign policy
decisions he made simply reflected the fact that his country was
isolated and surrounded by hostile capitalist countries, some of
which were supporting the Whites in the Civil War then raging
across his country. Foreign policy was a low-key issue and this was
reflected in the fact that the head of the Commissariat for Foreign
Affairs was Georgi Chicherin, a little-known diplomat of noble birth,

whilst his deputy, Maxim Litvinov, had fled from Russia after taking an active part in the events of 1905 and for some years had lived in exile in Britain. Neither Chicherin nor Litvinov were members of the decision-making Politburo and, prior to 1925, were not even represented on the Communist Party's Central Committee. Lenin had good reason to hope that the success of the Bolshevik revolution in Russia might set an example and lead to similar insurrections elsewhere. Certainly, for a time, there seemed every possibility of uprisings in Germany and Hungary. In Germany, the state of Bavaria had declared itself a Soviet Republic and, in January 1919, revolutionaries known as Spartacists had attempted a coup whilst in Hungary, the revolutionary Bela Kun had successfully set up a Communist regime. Both were short lived and brutally put down and afterwards enthusiasm for revolution died away and Europe settled into a more stable period. In 1920, Lenin seemed to indicate his willingness to resume normal methods of diplomacy with other countries when he said, 'We have entered a new period in which we...have won the right to our international existence in a network of capitalist states.'

The failure of attempted Communist coups in Germany and Hungary and general decline in revolutionary zeal suggested to the Soviet leaders that the chance of other sympathetic revolutions in Europe had gone and that the best interests of the new Bolshevik regime would be served in reaching agreement and co-operating with the capitalist countries. This was intended to be a short-term measure and would not prevent them from working behind the scenes to infiltrate, subvert and use Communist propaganda as a means of overthrowing capitalism elsewhere. To start with, their main means of achieving this would be through Comintern.

The Third International – Comintern

Comintern, the abbreviated form of Communist International, was founded in Moscow in March 1919 as a successor to the 2nd Socialist International. With the declared aim of sponsoring and supporting world revolution, at its Second Congress in 1921 it set down conditions for membership that effectively gave the leadership of the movement to the Soviet Union. Members had to accept all Comintern policy decisions and, when instructed, attempt to infiltrate the political systems of other countries and take advantage of democratic institutions then use them to overthrow governments. The language of Comintern was German since it was at first assumed that a socialist revolution was about to be successful there. Lenin always delivered his speeches in German and he hoped to transfer the headquarters of the organization to Berlin. As we shall see, the activities of Comintern infuriated foreign powers particularly since the Soviet Union claimed that it was only a member of Comintern and did not control its activities. The policy of the Soviet government appeared ambiguous since on the one hand it sought to establish diplomatic relations with the capitalist nations but on the other hand seemed dedicated to the cause of revolution and the overthrow of their democratically elected governments. Once Lenin's hopes had failed to materialize because of the failure of the Spartacist uprising in Germany in 1919, and as the political situation in post-war Europe stabilized, so the influence of Comintern lessened though it still remained a cornerstone of Soviet foreign policy.

Even though the Bolsheviks had supported the Spartacist-led attempted Communist coup in Germany, the new socialist-led government of the German Weimar Republic had much in common with the Soviet Union. Lenin was unusually prophetic when he summed up the situation:

> *Germany wants revenge and we want revolution. For the moment, our aims are the same...but when our ways part, they will be our most ferocious enemies. Time will tell whether German authority or Communism is to arise out of the ruins of Europe.*

For different reasons, both Bolshevik Russia and Weimar Germany were considered 'pariah nations' and were treated as outcasts. Russia, considered the 'hotbed of Bolshevism and revolution' and Germany, held responsible for starting the suffering of the First World War, were both denied membership of the League of Nations and kept isolated from mainstream European affairs. Both countries also resented the fact that, as part of the post-war settlement, they had lost territory to create Poland. For these reasons and the fact that Russian leaders feared the setting up of an anti-Soviet alliance, Lenin looked for closer ties with Germany and, in 1922, the two countries signed the Treaty of Rapallo.

The Treaty of Rapallo, 1922*

The treaty brought about the restoration of diplomatic relations between the two countries and they also agreed to drop any outstanding reparation claims they had against each other and pledged economic co-operation. Links were also established between the Red Army and the German army, the *Reichswehr*, and although expressly forbidden by the terms of the Treaty of Versailles, secret arrangements were made for German troops to take part in exercises on Soviet soil and for German engineers to manufacture and test new weapons. It was during this time that many German pilots, later to fly the bombers of the German air force, the *Luftwaffe*, received their initial training. Of course, from a Russian viewpoint, this gave them the advantage of access to German military technology. Much to the annoyance of Britain and France, the Treaty of Rapallo led to five years of good Soviet–German relations but Russia's relations with other European powers did not run so smoothly.

As the 1920s progressed, some attempt was made to rehabilitate the Soviet Union and restore her to the European family of nations. For his part, Lenin was keen to resume trade with the capitalist countries in order to buy essential modern machinery and find markets for her exports that would allow her to earn much needed foreign currency. In 1921, the first to establish diplomatic relations with the Communist regime were Russia's immediate neighbours, the Baltic States of Estonia, Latvia and Lithuania and they were soon followed by Finland. The Treaty of Riga, signed in 1921, finally settled the border between Russia and Poland and this allowed diplomatic relations to be established between the two countries.

At the Genoa Conference in 1922, Britain and France offered credit and loans to the Soviet government but only on condition that they settled outstanding debts dating back to tsarist times as well as restore to their owners foreign property and businesses that had been confiscated at the time of the Revolution. These demands Georgi Chicherin refused to even consider.

Even though a trade treaty was signed between Britain and the Soviet Union in 1921, many issues continued to hinder the restoration of

* Take care not to confuse this treaty with another Treaty of Rapallo, signed in 1920, that settled outstanding differences between Italy and Yugoslavia.

good relations between the two countries. In the first place and in common with other countries, the British government remained suspicious of Russian intentions particularly since Soviet propaganda was encouraging unrest in British India. In spite of this, in 1924, Ramsay MacDonald's First Labour Government recognized Russia's Communist regime. In October of the same year and at the height of an election campaign, the *Daily Mail* and other newspapers published a letter allegedly signed by Grigory Zinoviev, a Politburo member and chairman of Comintern, encouraging acts of mutiny in the British army. The letter, which may have been a forgery, led to a so-called 'Red Scare' and had the effect of rallying support for the opposition parties. This largely contributed to the failure of the short-lived Labour government to win the election. There were those who were convinced the letter was a forgery planted to ensure the return of a Conservative government whilst others believe it may have been the work of émigré organizations based in Britain. In spite of this, the following year Mikhail Tomsk, head of the Soviet trade union movement and a member of the Politburo, was invited to address the British Trade Union Congress. During 1926, the year of the General Strike in Britain, Comintern agents were suspected of being involved in subversive activities and in 1927, relations reached rock bottom when police raided the offices of *Arcos*, a Russian trading organization based in London, and found subversive material. As a result, the British government broke off diplomatic relations with the Soviet Union and these were not resumed until 1930.

As with Britain, it was the Russian refusal to settle tsarist debts that soured relations with France. Between 1894 and 1914, some 2 million French people had invested heavily in Russian bonds that under the Communist regime had become worthless. In spite of this, in 1924 France finally recognized the Soviet Union. In 1923, the murder of a Russian diplomat, Vatslav Vorovky, in Lausanne embittered relations between the Soviet Union and Switzerland.

Soviet opportunities in the Far East

Beyond Europe, the country that appeared to offer the Soviet Union's Communist regime with the greatest opportunity to extend her influence was China. In 1911, Chinese nationalist revolutionaries, known as the *Kuomintang* or KMT, finally overthrew the Manchu dynasty that had ruled China for nearly 300 years. The leader of the movement, Sun Yat-sen, formerly a Hong Kong trained doctor, then turned China into a republic. After his death in 1925, the leadership of the Kuomintang passed to Chiang Kai-shek but from the start, his rule was challenged by the Chinese Communists led by Mao Zedong who set up a Communist republic in the province of Kiangsi. During the conflict between Chiang Kai-shek's Kuomintang and Mao's Communists, the Soviet Union played a cunning game by backing both sides. Whilst Stalin sent material aid to the Chinese Communists, he also sent Mikhail Borodin, a Cominform agent who had earlier spent over ten years living in exile in the United States, to serve as a military adviser to the Nationalists. Trotsky was unhappy with this ploy and warned against becoming too involved in Chinese affairs since it might attract the attention of other world powers and encourage the involvement of Japan. At the Communist Party Congress held in Moscow in 1927, Stalin told delegates that he regarded China as 'the second home of world revolution' and confided that he intended to use Chiang Kai-shek's Kuomintang to his own advantage and 'squeeze them like a lemon' before abandoning them. In fact, the Russian leader had badly underrated Chiang and in so doing, supported the wrong side. During 1927, the Chinese Nationalists captured Shanghai, massacred all the Communists in the city and forced what remained of Mao's forces to flee into the hills where, continually harassed, they embarked on a 13,000-kilometre journey to find sanctuary in distant Shensi province. In Chinese history, this perilous epic journey is known as the 'Long March'. The failure of Stalin's policy for China led to much soul-searching in Moscow as members of the Politburo sought to apportion blame. Trotsky held Stalin and Bukharin responsible for the catastrophe and, as we saw earlier, this was the time when Stalin reacted by expelling his critics from the Party.

The late 1920s witnessed attempts to ease international tension and so improve the chances of securing a lasting peace in Europe. In 1925, European leaders attended a conference at Locarno in Italy to try to settle outstanding disputes. At the conference, a major role was played by the German representative, Gustav Stresemann, who agreed to accept Germany's western frontiers as final but wanted, at some time in the future, to re-negotiate Germany's frontiers in the east with Poland and Czechoslovakia. The Soviet Union was not involved in these decisions but, the following year, further improved her relations with Germany by signing the Treaty of Berlin. By the terms of this treaty, both countries pledged to remain neutral in the event of an attack by another power. 1926 also saw the signing of the Kellogg-Briand Pact that renounced war as a means of settling international disputes. The signatories to the Pact were Britain, France, Germany, Italy, Japan and the United States but again the Soviet Union was uninvolved. In the same year the Soviet diplomat, Teodor Nette, was murdered in a train at Riga in Latvia. Overall, 1927 was if anything an even worse year for Soviet diplomacy. Canada joined Britain in breaking off diplomatic relations whilst in Warsaw, yet another Soviet diplomat was assassinated, this time their ambassador to Poland. The problem was that whilst Stalin wanted to be more involved in European politics, the activities of Comintern and his own utterances meant that few trusted him and consequently the Soviet Union was sidelined. However, the rise to power of Adolf Hitler and the Nazi Party in Germany was soon to change the situation completely.

Challenges to Soviet diplomacy in the 1930s

Adolf Hitler, who described Bolshevism as the 'arch enemy of civilization', had always been a bitter opponent and outspoken critic of Soviet Communism. In *Mein Kampf*, he had openly stated that the additional living space or *lebensraum* needed by Germany would have to be obtained in eastern Europe and largely at the expense of Russia. Maxim Litvinov, deputy Commissariat for Foreign Affairs, now realized that his country's best guarantee of safety from possible German aggression would be to enter into pacts with other nations and so gain the advantage of collective security – safety in numbers. In what became known as the Litvinov Protocol, the Soviet Union agreed a series of non-aggression pacts with France, Poland, Finland and Estonia in 1933, with Italy in 1934 and with Czechoslovakia in 1936. Britain played no part in these arrangements and much to Stalin's concern, had, in 1935, entered into an agreement with Germany – the Anglo-German Naval Agreement. This made the Soviet leader very suspicious of Britain's long-term intentions.

From its inception in 1919, Lenin had shown no enthusiasm for the League of Nations, the international organization set up after the

First World War to preserve the peace and arrange the settlement of disputes through arbitration. Whilst Litvinov also spoke of it in the most scathing terms, the Bolshevik leader described it as 'a band of robbers.' Very gradually as Russia became involved in some of the League's projects, Lenin changed his mind and, in 1927, Russian delegates attended an economic conference organized by the League and Litvinov took part in disarmament talks held at Geneva. Finally, as evidence of her new found respectability, the Soviet Union joined the League of Nations in 1934 and was elected to the all-important Council which met when there was an emergency to be dealt with.

Not only did Stalin have a reason to be worried about Hitler's ambitions in Europe, he also had good cause to be worried about developments in the Far East. When the Japanese began to show interest in expanding into Outer Mongolia and Manchuria, he had tried to buy them off by offering mineral and fishing rights and selling them the Chinese Eastern Railway. This ploy was only successful for a while and during 1937 tension mounted and there were numerous incidents along the Manchurian border. From time to time, there were frequent clashes between Russian and Japanese forces, any one of which might have turned into a full-scale war – a war for which the Soviet Union was by no means prepared.

In Europe, the years 1934 and 1935 witnessed significant changes in international relationships that led to dangerous shifts in the balance of power. In 1934, Germany and Poland agreed a ten-year Non-Aggression Pact that Hitler claimed would begin a new chapter of peaceful development in Polish-German relations. The Pact, the first by any country with Nazi Germany, suggested that Germany had no quarrel with Poland. This came as a surprise to Stalin and effectively brought to an end the period of the Soviet Union's good relations with Germany. It caused him to press further ahead in his attempt to enter into alliances that offered collective security. In 1935, Russia made pacts of mutual assistance with France and Czechoslovakia and the following year agreed a Non-Aggression Pact with China.

In October of that year, the Italian dictator, Benito Mussolini, ordered the invasion of the independent African state of Abyssinia, present-day Ethiopia. The move was severely criticized by the League of Nations and Mussolini's allies, Britain and France, and as a result, he withdrew Italy from membership of the League and instead looked for closer ties with Nazi Germany. Italy's Fascist leader spoke of 'the Rome–Berlin lines…an axis, around which can revolve all those European states with a will to collaboration and peace'. So it was that Nazi Germany and Fascist Italy became known as the 'Axis powers', a name they would retain during the Second World War. Stalin's concern at these developments was further heightened when, in 1936, Germany and Japan agreed an Anti-Comintern Pact.

The Anti-Comintern Pact, 1936

The Anti-Comintern Pact, first agreed between Germany and Japan, was signed in Berlin in November 1936 and Italy joined a year later. As the title suggests, the declared aim of the Pact was 'to mutually keep each other informed concerning the activities of the Communist International' and 'to confer upon the necessary measures of defence'. It was also agreed to invite other nations 'menaced by the disintegrating work of the Communist International' to join the Pact. Stalin can hardly have been surprised by the steps taken against a movement whose declared aim was to sponsor and support world revolution! Whilst the aim of the Anti-Comintern Pact was to counter the activities of Comintern, there can be little doubt that it was specifically aimed at the Soviet Union. Hitler had often raged against Russian Communism that he regarded as a Bolshevik-Jewish plot to win world domination. The Japanese leaders, already upset by the Soviet-Chinese Non-Aggression Treaty, were further angered to discover that the Soviet Union had been secretly selling aircraft and weapons to China. Mussolini stated that Italy had joined the Anti-Comintern Pact in order 'to defend Western values against the threat of Soviet Communism'.

The problem faced by the Soviet Union was that although Stalin appeared to have abandoned his revolutionary aims and had introduced a constitution which, at least on the face of it, seemed reasonably democratic, the Western powers were still suspicious of his motives. The question was, could he really be trusted? With Germany and Italy now firmly opposed, France was uncertain and Britain was not prepared to give Stalin the benefit of the doubt. Rather late in the day, the Soviet Union dropped its opposition to moderate socialism and urged communists and socialists of all persuasions to form 'popular front' governments. In July 1936, a civil war broke out in Spain.

The involvement of the Soviet Union in the Spanish Civil War

In February 1936, the Spanish people went to the polls and elected a republican, left-wing, National Front government under Manuel Azana. His government promised to enact a series of much needed social reforms. The election result concerned conservative elements in the country and members of the Spanish Fascist Party, the Falange, reacted by stirring up riots and carrying out political assassinations. Soon there was widespread violence as Falangists and Communists fought openly in the streets and exchanged murder for murder and outrage for outrage. Additional anxiety was caused by the anti-clerical activities of Spanish Communists that took the form of savage attacks on priests and nuns and destroyed church property. In July, the Spanish army in Morocco mutinied and, led by the popular general, Jose Sanjurjo, crossed to the mainland with the intention of overthrowing the government. Another general, Francisco Franco, also transferred his army to the mainland, joined Sanjurjo, and advanced to meet government forces. The civil war that followed was to become 'the ideological battleground of Europe'. On the one side were those who supported the legitimate Spanish government, the Republicans, and these included socialists, communists andmost of the urban working class as well as agricultural workers; on the other side were the Nationalists, who had the support of most of the upper and middle classes, the landowners, industrialists and those with banking and commercial interests, the Church, the Falange Party and most significant of all, the Spanish army.

From the start, there was outside intervention and even though foreign powers did not appear to be directly involved, both sides attracted the support of overseas sympathizers. The Nationalists received military aid from Italy and Germany with Italy sending 75,000 men and large amounts of weapons and Germany, 17,000 men and squadrons of aircraft. The most famous of these was the Condor Squadron that, on 26 April 1937, carried out an attack against the Basque town of Guernica that led to the deaths of 1,600 men, women and children. This, the first use of a form of aerial bombardment to be known as *blitzkrieg*, led to an outcry and caused the famous Spanish artist, Pablo Picasso, to paint *Guernica* portraying the horror of the event. Stalin had to play his hand carefully since he did not want to risk a direct confrontation with Germany and Italy. The view has long been held that Soviet contribution to the civil war, in terms of men and materials, was far less than that of Italy and Germany but recent research has shown this to be untrue.

In addition, Stalin also sanctioned the involvement of Comintern and sent Soviet military advisers to assist the Republican army. Comintern agents helped to recruit overseas volunteers to fight alongside the Republicans and these units, known as the International Brigade, were to play an important part in the war. The involvement of Comintern did not end there since their agents tried to influence the conduct of the war and become involved in Spanish politics. They also urged the Communists to turn on the Spanish socialists and Trotskyists and organized their mass executions. These activities, together with the intrigues between the various sections on the Republican side, contributed to the ultimate victory of Franco's Nationalists early in 1939.

During this period, there were further ominous signs of Nazi German's belligerent intentions. In March 1936, Hitler defied the terms of the Treaty of Versailles when he ordered German troops to re-occupy the Rhineland. The Rhineland, originally a part of Germany, had been occupied by British and French troops and declared a demilitarized zone. France wanted to act but in Britain there was some sympathy for the German action since, according to some, they 'were only going into their own back garden'. As early as 1934, Hitler had tried to bring about the union of Germany with

Table 9.1   The extent of foreign involvement in the Spanish Civil War

	Men	Tanks	Artillery	Planes
Italy	75,000	150	1,000	660
Germany	17,000	200	1,000	600
Soviet Union	3,000	900	1,550	10,000

Austria, the *Anschluss*, but had been prevented by Mussolini. With Italy now an ally of Germany, the situation had changed and, in March 1938, the Nazi leader tried again and this time was successful. The Nazi leader next turned his attention to Czechoslovakia.

The Soviet Union and the Czech crisis

Czechoslovakia, newly created in 1919 following the break-up of the old Empire of Austria-Hungary, had emerged as one of the most democratic and prosperous countries in Europe. Under the leadership of Tomas Masaryk the small republic, situated in central Europe with a long common border with Germany, had managed to safeguard the identity and interests of the races – Czechs, Slovaks, Bohemians and Moravians – who lived within her frontiers. In spite of this, the Czechs and Slovaks made uneasy bedfellows but Masaryk and his close friend, Eduard Benes, had been able to maintain racial harmony. Along the German border was a region known as the Sudetenland whose population included 3 million Germans. Under the leadership of Konrad Henlein who had formed a Nazi-type Sudeten German Party, the Sudeten Germans complained of the hardships and injustices of living under Czech rule. Using pro-German propaganda, they became more demanding and restless as they campaigned for their independence and union with Germany. In April 1938, rumours of German troops' movements along the Czech frontier led to panic and it seemed that a European war was imminent. Although France and the Soviet Union had entered into agreements to guarantee Czech independence, it was the British prime minister, Neville Chamberlain, who took steps to try to resolve the situation. Two meetings with Hitler at Berchtesgaden and Godesberg failed to find a solution but at a third held at Munich in September, Chamberlain and the French prime minister, Eduard Daladier, finally gave in to Hitler's demands. Many regarded the surrender of the Sudetenland to Germany as an act of appeasement and a betrayal of Czechoslovakia.

During the crisis, the Soviet Union repeatedly proposed international action to deter Hitler's aggression but this went unheeded. Stalin grew increasingly concerned at the turn of events since Litvinov's attempt to create a system of alliances and bring Russia within a protective framework of collective security appeared to have failed. In May 1939, Stalin replaced Litvinov with Vyacheslav Molotov.

1922	Treaty of Rapallo with Germany
1925	Trade treaty with Germany
	Treaty of Friendship with Turkey
1926	Treaty of Friendship with Lithuania
1927	Treaty of Friendship with Persia
1931	Non-aggression pact with Afghanistan
1932	Non-aggression pacts with Finland, Latvia, Estonia, Poland and France
1933	Diplomatic relations established with the United States
1934	Soviet Union joined the League of Nations
1936	Pacts of mutual assistance with France and Czechoslovakia

Born Vyacheslav Skriabin and related to the famous Russian composer Alexander Skriabin, Molotov had long been involved in revolutionary activities. He joined the Bolsheviks in 1909 and took the name 'Molotov' which means 'hammer' and after working on the newspaper *Pravda*, he became the youngest member of the Politburo. After the death of Lenin, he became one of the staunchest supporters of Stalin and was rewarded for his loyalty with a string of appointments until, in May 1939, he replaced Litvinov as Soviet Commissar for Foreign Affairs. In May 1939, the new Soviet foreign secretary secretly contacted the Germans about the possibility of agreeing a non-aggression pact between the two countries.

The German–Soviet Non-Aggression Pact of August 1939

When the German delegates arrived in Moscow, there was already an Anglo-French mission there trying to reach an agreement with the Russians. They were suddenly told that the talks were to be adjourned and sent home and instead Molotov opened negotiations with the Germans. The agreement reached, usually called the German-Soviet Pact, is also sometimes referred to as the

Ribbentrop-Molotov Pact, after the names of the two signatories. The pact consisted of two agreements: one dealt with economic matters and the other, a non-aggression pact, was signed four days later. The economic agreement provided for the supply of Russian food products and raw materials in exchange for German manufactured goods and machinery. The non-aggression pact publicly stated that Germany and Russia would never attack one another and that any problems arising between them would be settled amicably. The pact between the two countries with two totally opposed ideologies was intended to last for ten years.

Wonder how long the honeymoon will last?
Clifford Berryman's cartoon that appeared in the Washington Post on 9 October 1939.

Whilst it amazed the rest of the world, few thought it would last and was recognized as being nothing more than a marriage of convenience – an arrangement brought about because it was convenient to both sides at the time.

As far as Germany was concerned, the German-Soviet Pact meant that the Soviet Union would not stand in the way if Germany invaded Poland. Further, if France and Britain stood by Poland, Russia would stand aside and not become involved in the war and this would spare

Germany the prospect of having to fight a war on two fronts. From Stalin's point of view, the Pact offered some respite from the threat of a German invasion and gave time for his country to prepare for a war that now seemed inevitable.

A secret protocol or addition to the Pact was the arrangement for the future partition of Poland between the two countries and, as a reward for agreeing not to become involved in a future war, Germany agreed that the Soviet Union could occupy the Baltic States – Latvia, Estonia and Lithuania. Fitzroy Maclean, a young British diplomat working in Russia at the time later wrote:

> *Stalin was being offered on the one hand by Hitler what he hoped meant peace, which he needed very badly to pull the Soviet Union together, plus very considerable territorial gains, the Baltic States, half of Poland, Finland, odd bits of the Balkans, all for keeping out of the war, which he wanted to do anyway. We were offering him a front-line position in the nastiest war there had ever been. And that didn't appeal to him at all.*

From *Eastern Approaches* by Sir Fitzroy Maclean, 1950

The German–Soviet invasion of Poland

On 1 September 1939, German troops crossed the Polish frontier and were engaged in fierce fighting along the Westerplatte. The flat Polish plain was well suited to fast-moving tank units, Panzers, and with the support of the air force, the *Luftwaffe*, the Germans were able to advance rapidly across the country. Outnumbered and outgunned, the Poles fought a courageous rearguard action as they struggled to hold the *blitzkrieg* onslaught. On 3 September, after Hitler chose to ignore an ultimatum demanding the withdrawal of German forces from Poland, Britain and France declared war on Germany and the Second World War began in earnest. In accordance with the terms of the German-Soviet Pact, on 17 September Soviet troops entered eastern Poland and advanced to the line agreed in the secret protocol. The occupied territory now became a part of the Western Ukraine and Western Byelorussia. With the Red Army came the political commissars and the NKVD to begin imposing Stalinist-Communism on the people. A great many atrocities were committed against the Polish people with the worst of these being the mass murder of over 4,000 Polish army officers in a wood at Katyn, near Smolensk. Their mass grave was discovered by invading German soldiers in 1943 and Nazi officials immediately accused the Russians of the massacre. The Soviet authorities denied this and made a counter claim that the Germans were trying to cover up their own atrocity. It was not until 1990 that the then Soviet leader, Mikhail Gorbachev, admitted Russian responsibility. Molotov later referred to the Soviet invasion of Poland and boasted to the Supreme Soviet that the Red Army had finally destroyed 'the misshapen offspring of the Versailles Treaty'. Ten days later, Molotov and Ribbentrop met to formalize the partition of Poland, agree the new frontier between the two countries and arrange for Germans living in eastern Poland to return to Hitler's *Reich*. During the weeks that followed, the Baltic States were each made to sign treaties that allowed Soviet troops to be stationed within their borders and so, to all intents and purpose, lost their independence. Finland, however, stood firm against Stalin's demands and refused to hand over land on the Karelian Isthmus, which the Russians needed to protect the approaches to the port of Leningrad and make it less vulnerable to German attack. They also demanded the demilitarization of the Mannerheim Line, a line of fortifications across the Karelian Isthmus, rights to lease the Finnish port of Hanko and use it as a naval base and the surrender of several islands in the Gulf of Finland. Stalin took it as an affront when the Finnish government refused to accede to these demands and scrapped the non-aggression agreed between the two countries in 1932. Shortly after, the Soviet leader broke off diplomatic relations with Finland, accusing Finnish soldiers of firing on a village close to their common frontier. Finally, on 30 November 1939, Russian forces invaded Finland and Molotov declared the country to be under the control of a new Finnish People's Government led by the socialist and intellectual, Otto Kuusinen, who was prepared to govern as Stalin's puppet. As Molotov was soon to find out, he was speaking prematurely!

The Russo-Finnish war – the 'Winter War' of 1939–40

When the Russians invaded Finland, they quickly discovered that they had taken on more than they had bargained for. The Red Army, short of experienced officers as a result of Stalin's purges, failed to win its expected easy victory and much to Stalin's annoyance and embarrassment 'the Russian steamroller army failed to roll'. In fact, the Finnish soldiers proved themselves superior to their Russian counterparts in winter warfare and from their defensive positions along the Mannerheim Line checked the advance of the Red Army and inflicted 200,000 casualties on the invaders.

Thursday, November 30, 1939, "South Wales Echo & Express."

BIG-HEARTED MARTYR

FINLAND

STALIN : Now, be fair, madam ! Didn't I try to persuade the landlord to let me in without disturbing you ?

A J.C. Walker cartoon that appeared in the South Wales Echo on 30 November 1939 shows Stalin trying to excuse his invasion of Finland.

The bravery of the Finns attracted the admiration of other nations and whilst Sweden and Norway sent volunteers to help defend their neighbour, Britain and France provided military aid. However, faced by overwhelming odds, their resistance collapsed and they were forced to surrender. By the terms of the Treaty of Moscow, Finland was forced to surrender some 40,000 square kilometres of land including part of the Karelian Isthmus, the port of Vyborg and other territory in the north including the Petsamo region. This now gave the Soviet Union a common frontier with Norway. Even so, Finland's contribution to the war was not over. Stalin next exerted additional pressure on the Baltic States and insisted that they appointed governments that 'coincided with Soviet interests'. By this he meant that the three countries had to become Soviet-style republics and in August 1940 were finally annexed by the Soviet Union.

Meanwhile in Europe, the war was going badly for Britain and France. After the defeat of Poland, there was a lull, a 'Phoney War', during which action was limited to patrol activity along the Western Front. Hitler even started a 'peace offensive' and tried to woo the Allies by claiming that he harboured no ill will and had no further territorial claims to make. In April 1940, the 'Phoney War' ended suddenly when German troops occupied Denmark and Norway and then, in May, Hitler's offensive in the West began with the invasion of Belgium and the Netherlands and a speedy advance through north-eastern France. As the situation became critical, so Winston Churchill became the British prime minister. As France tottered before the advancing German armies, units of the British and French armies were surrounded in a pocket close to the ports of Calais and Dunkirk. The rescue of over 338,000 men from the beaches could not delay the inevitable and on 22 June 1940, after what was no more than a six-weeks offensive, France finally surrendered. During this time, Mussolini had found the courage to bring Italy into the war on Germany's side. Now Britain stood alone, backed only by servicemen from the Commonwealth and thousands who had fled from German-occupied Europe determined to continue the fight to liberate their homelands.

Stalin, determined not to be outdone by Hitler's successes in the West, demanded that Romania surrendered the provinces of Bessarabia and Bukovina and when this was refused, the Red Army occupied these regions. Even though the German victory over France brought a letter of congratulation from Molotov, and in spite of the understanding reached by the German-Soviet Pact, relations between the two countries began to worsen. Towards the end of 1940, Molotov travelled to Berlin to seek German agreement for the Soviet Union to complete the invasion of Finland and, in addition, occupy Romania and Bulgaria. The Germans would have none of it and fobbed him off with vague promises of parts of the British Empire once the British had been defeated. The truth was that 'on the chessboard that was the map of Europe, Hitler held all the major pieces and Stalin only a handful of pawns'. Barely a month later, Hitler signed Order Number 2 that sanctioned preparations for the invasion of Russia.

Stalin was not oblivious to what was going on and as the Soviet armaments industry worked flat out to equip the country's standing army of 4 million men, Molotov intensified his search for allies. Clearly it was an act of desperation when in 1940, Russia agreed a treaty of neutrality with Japan, a country that in 1936 had joined Germany in the Anti-Comintern Pact! It did, however, guarantee that if war came, the Soviet Union would not have to fight on two fronts – against Germany in the West and Japan in the East.

In April 1941, Hitler delayed his proposed attack on Russia and invaded Yugoslavia instead but this did not prevent the intensifying of her military preparations and by mid-June the German armies were ready to move. At this point Stalin appeared to be behaving very strangely since, although he accepted that a future war with Germany was inevitable, he refused to believe warnings that a German onslaught was imminent even though German reconnaissance aircraft were flying quite openly over Rusian territory. Warnings came not only from Winston Churchill but from his own ace spy, Victor Sorge. Sorge, who had a German father and a Russian mother, was a dedicated Communist and a master linguist. A member of the worldwide Soviet espionage network, he had worked in Britain, the United States and Germany and, whilst in Germany, had even masqueraded as a member of the Nazi Party. He supplied Moscow with a stream of useful information including the date of the intended German invasion. Stalin refused to believe him and seemed certain that Hitler would never go back on the undertakings of the Non-Aggression Pact of 1939. Even more bizarre was the fact that a German soldier, Alfred Liskow, went over to the Russians and gave them details and the exact date of the invasion. Stalin had him shot for spreading rumours! In an attempt to clarify the situation, a meeting was arranged between Ribbentrop, the German foreign minister, and Vladimir Dekanozov, the Russian ambassador:

> *The Ambassador began by complaining about German violations of Soviet air space but Ribbentrop cut him short with the words – 'That is not the question now. The Soviet Government's hostile attitude to Germany and the serious threat represented by Russian troops on Germany's eastern frontier have compelled the Reich to take military counter measures.' He then read a list of alleged Soviet misdemeanours concluding, 'I myself have come to the conclusion that, in spite of serious endeavours, I have not succeeded in establishing reasonable relations between our two countries.' The Russian expressed regret...and left without shaking hands.*

> From *Ribbentrop* by Michael Bloch, 1993

At 4.15 a.m. on Sunday 22 June 1941, German armies invaded the Soviet Union.

10

The Great Patriotic War, 1941–5

This chapter will cover:
- *the reasons for the German invasion of Russia in 1941*
- *Operation Barbarossa*
- *the early stages of the war*
- *the significance of the Battles of Stalingrad and Kursk*
- *the Soviet Union under German occupation*
- *the Soviet wartime economy*
- *an assessment of the Soviet contribution to the Allied victory.*

> *Surrender is forbidden. VIth Army will hold their positions to the last man and the last round.*
>
> Hitler's orders to the German Army trapped at Stalingrad in 1943

Why did Hitler invade the Soviet Union?

There were two major reasons why Hitler ordered the invasion of the Soviet Union in June 1941. Firstly, Hitler's creed of National Socialism was directly opposed to Marxism and he made no secret of his loathing of Soviet Communism and his intention of destroying it. In *Mein Kampf*, he described Bolshevism as 'an infamous crime against humanity' and later in a speech said 'Bolshevism is the doctrine of the people who are lowest in the scale of civilization.' Although Germany had not yet defeated Britain, by the end of 1940 Hitler's growing impatience was obvious when he said, 'Russia's destruction must be made part of the struggle…The sooner Russia is crushed the better.' Secondly, Hitler had promised the German people *lebensraum* – adequate living space – and openly stated, 'If new territory is to be acquired, it must be mainly at Russia's cost.' The regions he sought to annex were White Russia, present-day Belarus, and the Ukraine.

Other reasons included the fact that many of the raw materials Germany needed in order to achieve *autarky*, self-sufficiency, were available in Russia. The Ukraine, sometimes referred to as 'the bread basket of Europe', would supply Germany with adequate grain reserves or, as Hitler bluntly put it, 'We will acquire soil for the German plough by the use of German steel and thus provide the nation with its daily bread.' To the south lay the oil-rich Caucasus that would ensure the mobility of the German armed forces in a future war, and elsewhere across Russia lay vast resources of coal and a host of other minerals. The acquisition of Russia would also place millions of Jews within Hitler's grasp. You will recall that he considered Marxism as being part of a Jewish conspiracy to achieve world domination and he now claimed to possess irrefutable evidence to back this up. He made clear his intentions when he said, 'Either they pass over our bodies or we over theirs!' Hitler also doubted Stalin's good faith and believed that it was essential for Germany to strike first before Russian economic and military might was sufficient to pose a real threat. With regard to the war, he calculated that the invasion of the Soviet Union would lead to the collapse of Britain. He had earlier commented, 'Britain's hope lies with Russia...If Russia drops out of the war, all is lost for Britain...'.

Operation Barbarossa

Operation Barbarossa was the code-name given to the German plans for the invasion of Russia. It was taken from the name of a legendary German hero, the former Emperor of the Holy Roman Empire, Frederick I, who was better known as Barbarossa or 'red beard'. Hitler had boasted, 'When Operation Barbarossa is launched, the world will hold its breath,' and added, 'We will only have to kick in the front door and the whole rotten edifice will come tumbling down.' Of course, he had good reason to believe in an easy German victory since his armies had won spectacular victories in Poland and France, whilst against Finland, the Red Army's performance had been less than impressive.

Finally, after a five-week delay, on the morning of 22 June 1941 more than 3 million German troops backed by Panzer units consisting of 3,350 tanks and massed formations of aircraft began the invasion of the Soviet Union along a 3,200-kilometre front that stretched from the Baltic Sea in the north to the Black Sea in the south. That morning, Molotov broadcast to the Russian people:

> *Today, without any claims having been presented to the Soviet Union, without declaration of war, German troops have attacked our country... This unheard of attack upon our country is a betrayal unparalleled in the history of civilized nations. The attack on our country was carried out despite the fact that a treaty of non-aggression had been signed between the USSR and Germany... Entire responsibility for the attack falls fully and completely upon the German Fascist rulers. The war has been forced upon us, not by the German people, not by German workers... but by the clique of bloodthirsty Fascist rulers of Germany... The government calls upon you to rally closely around our glorious Bolshevik Party, around our great leader and comrade, Stalin. Ours is a righteous cause. The enemy shall be defeated. Victory will be ours.*

On 26 June, Finland declared war on the Soviet Union to be followed the next day by Hungary. In July, Britain and Russia signed a mutual aid agreement and both countries undertook not to make a separate peace with Germany.

For the invasion of Russia, the German armies, which included Romanians, Hungarians and Italians, were divided into three Army Groups. Each was to be part of a three-pronged drive deep into the Soviet Union and each had specific objectives. Army Group North was to advance through the Baltic States towards Leningrad; Army Group Centre was to move due east and after capturing Minsk and Smolensk, head towards Moscow; Army Group South was to pass through the Ukraine, cross the River Dnepr and then head towards Kharkov.

During the first weeks of the campaign, the German armies made impressive progress as their Panzers raced forward along the length of the front. The resistance offered by the Red Army was spasmodic with some units fighting bravely and others retreating to leave the Germans unopposed. The ferocity of the German attack was such that at the end of three weeks Army Group Centre alone had taken over 300,000 prisoners, 2,500 tanks and masses of military equipment. By early August, the Russians had surrendered all the Polish territory they had occupied in 1939 and the Germans were at the gates of Leningrad where the people were about to begin the horrors of a

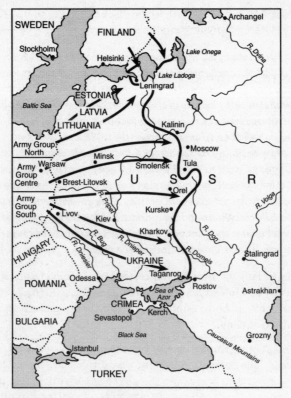

Figure 10.1 'Barbarossa' – the German invasion of Russia.

900-day siege. To the south, Minsk and Smolensk were quickly occupied and the Germans were across the River Dnieper and at the end of September, the Army Group Centre launched Operation Typhoon, an all-out offensive intended to capture Moscow. By this time, Russian resistance had stiffened but even so the Germans were able to reach the suburbs of the city before fierce counter-attacks forced them to retreat. During this period, Stalin remained in Moscow but the remainder of the Soviet government moved eastward to find safety in Kuybyshev (present-day Samara), an industrial city in south-central European Russia on the banks of the River Volga.

In some regions such as the Baltic States and the Ukraine the advancing Germans were regarded as liberators and thousands were prepared to collaborate and even form units to fight alongside the invaders. The onset of winter slowed the German advance and by the end of 1941 Leningrad and Moscow were still in Russian hands but

Hitler's hopes of achieving an outright victory by the end of the year had not materialized. What had gone wrong?

The German offensive – what went wrong?

Hitler's decision to invade Russia in June 1941 before he had defeated Britain meant that he had to maintain sizeable forces in the west and this meant that Germany was faced with the prospect of fighting on two fronts. In addition, the German armies were further weakened by the need to divert units to other campaigns being fought in the Balkans and North Africa. Equally important was the fact that the five-week delay at the start of the offensive meant that the Germans had less time to gain their objectives before the onset of the Russian winter. It has also been claimed that Hitler ignored important intelligence about the deployment of Red Army units and that he was surprised by the bravery of the Russian soldiers. He commented, 'They fight with truly stupid fanaticism and with the primitive brutality of an animal that sees itself trapped.'

Of course, the reason why Russian soldiers fought with such fanaticism was that discipline in the Red Army was enforced by the NKVD who took immediate action against cowards, deserters and those whose morale appeared to be flagging. Again, as the Germans advanced deeper into the Soviet Union, so their lines of communication lengthened and this led to shortages of food, clothing and munitions. Any hope of using the Russian railways to transport materials forward to the front was prevented by the fact that the gauge of Russian railway lines differed from that of the German! To make matters worse, Stalin had ordered, 'Do not leave a single house, a single animal, a single grain of food' and this meant that as the Russians retreated, they carried out a 'scorched earth policy' destroying anything that might be of value to the Germans. Since they were more used to Russian winters, Red Army soldiers were better able to cope with the sub-zero temperatures which brought frostbite and even the fear of freezing to death. On their feet, Russian soldiers wore *valenki*, feltboots, as well as two pairs of woollen socks; on their heads they had hats over balaclava-type helmets. The Germans had none of these and some units possessed no winter clothing whatsoever, this meant that at night when temperatures fell to –44 °C, limbs first turned purple before stiffening with frostbite.

Adverse climatic conditions did not cease with the end of winter. Spring brought with it heavy rain that turned the roads to mud, making them impassible and clogging machinery. In the summer, men fighting in the Ukraine had to contend with scorching heat. There was always the fear of an attack by partisans, men who had formed resistance groups and continued to fight behind the German lines. The morale of German soldiers was also affected by rumours of what might befall them if they were taken prisoner by the Russians!

Leningrad – 'city of suffering and heroism'

Early in September 1941, the Germans and their Finnish allies completed the encirclement of Leningrad and the city was to remain beleaguered until its siege ended in January 1944, a total of 872 days. Around 2,887,000 Leningraders backed up by 200,000 Red Army soldiers would not consider surrendering 'the birthplace of the Revolution' and able-bodied men, women and children helped to dig anti-tank ditches and reinforce the city's defences. Even the composer Shostakovich was drafted into the service as a fire watcher and kept a lookout from the roof of the conservatory where he worked. It was during this time that he wrote his Seventh 'Leningrad' Symphony which was first performed in the besieged city. With sufficient fuel for only two months, no tapped water supplies, little electricity and little food, the defenders faced constant German bombing and shelling. At their lowest point, the bread ration was reduced to only 125 grammes a day. The only opportunity to escape from the city came in the winter when Lake Ladoga froze over and lorries were able to move across the ice on what became known as *Doroga Zhizni*, the 'Road of Life'. During the siege, the city's factories managed to produce munitions, students continued their studies and life went on as best as possible. During January and February 1942 alone, over 200,000 Leningraders died of cold and starvation and it has been estimated that during the siege some 800,000 people died and were buried in mass graves. The siege of the city finally ended on 17 January 1944 and after the war Leningrad was awarded the Order of Lenin and was the first to have the title Hero City bestowed on it.

A major change in the extent of the war came on 7 December 1941 when the Japanese attacked the American naval base of Pearl Harbor in the Hawaiian Islands. Shortly afterwards, Germany and Italy declared war on the United States. This turned a war that had been essentially a European war into a world war and meant that Britain, Russia and the United States were allies.

An early Russian offensive in the spring of 1942 was unsuccessful and a subsequent German counter-attack led to the encirclement and annihilation of the entire Soviet 33rd Army and afterwards, their disgraced commander, General Mikhail Efremov, took his own life. Then came the German summer offensive that was intended to make up for the failures of the previous year by taking Stalingrad on the River Volga, passing around the Sea of Azov and then advancing southwards to the oilfields of the Caucasus. During these months, the Red Army suffered over 4 million dead, wounded or taken prisoner whilst German losses were a relatively modest 1,150,000. On 19 November 1942, the Battle of Stalingrad began.

Figure 10.2 The Russian Front during 1942.

The Battle of Stalingrad – 'the Verdun of the Second World War'

It was on Hitler's orders that, in June, a German army of 330,000 men under General Friedrich von Paulus was diverted to take Stalingrad, an industrial city on the banks of the River Volga. It was intended that the army would take the city, cross the river and then sweep south towards the Caucasus and the Caspian Sea. The city also had the added attraction of being named after the Soviet leader. By the end of August, German troops had reached the river and fighting had started in the outskirts of the city and it was then that General Andrei Yeremonko, commander-in-chief of the Russians defending Stalingrad, issued an order:

> *Not one step back.*
>
> *The War Council expects unlimited courage, tenacity and heroism in the fight with the onrushing enemy from all fighters, commanders and political workers, from all the defenders of Stalingrad. The enemy must and will be smashed on the approaches to Stalingrad.*
>
> *Forward against the enemy. Up into the unrelenting battle, comrades, for Stalingrad, for our great country.*
>
> *Death to the German invaders.*

As Red Army soldiers contested every house and every street, the battle was to witness some of the fiercest hand-to-hand fighting of the war. An account written in the diary of Russian general, Vasili Chuikov, records:

> *We have fought during 15 days for a single house...And imagine Stalingrad – eight days and eight nights of hand-to-hand struggles. The street is no longer measured in metres but in corpses... Stalingrad is no longer a town. By day it is an enormous cloud of burning, blinding smoke. The nights of Stalingrad are a terror... animals flee this hell; the hardest stones cannot bear it for long; only men endure.*

Even so, the Germans succeeded in taking 80 per cent of the city before the Russian army commander, Marshal Georgi Zhukov, changed the battle plans. Aware that the most fanatical German units were spearheading their advance and that the flanks were protected by troops drawn from Italy, Romania and Hungary, he decided to attack at these points where the enemy appeared to be weakest. His plan was successful and as the enemy's line collapsed, so a pincer movement encircled von Paulus's army of men. The Germans fought bravely to hold their ground but as the situation became impossible, their commander asked permission for his men to fight their way out. Hitler refused, 'I am not leaving the Volga. The Sixth Army will do its historic duty at Stalingrad until the last man.' Thus he condemned his soldiers to fight to the bitter end – to the death. With food supplies and munitions running low and no chance of escape, von Paulus had no choice but to surrender. At Stalingrad, the Germans lost 147,000 men with a further 91,000 taken prisoner. The battle coincided with a British victory over the Germans at El Alamein in North Africa and, by proving that the German armies were not invincible, gave the Allies a new confidence. The battles turned out to be major turning points in the war.

Marshal Zhukov, a brilliant and decisive commander, still had a major role to play in the events leading to the end of the war. Amongst many other lesser-known figures was Vasily Zaitsev, a Red Army sniper who found the cover provided by the ruins of the city much to his liking and used his rifle equipped with telescopic sights to kill 232 of the enemy to became a national hero. Lilya Litvyak, aged 22 and a strikingly beautiful Russian fighter pilot, flew many sorties over the city to earn herself the nickname the 'White Rose of Stalingrad' but towards the end of the battle she was shot down and killed.

In spite of the defeat at Stalingrad, in February 1943 the Germans launched a spring offensive that held the Red Army advance towards the River Dnieper and forced it to retreat. To the north, the German armies on the Moscow front made a tactical retreat between Orel and Smolensk in order to shorten their line and improve their defensive positions whilst to the south, between Orel and Kharkov and towards Kursk, a bulge developed that extended 160 kilometres into the German lines. In order to eliminate this salient, the Germans made plans for Operation Citadel.

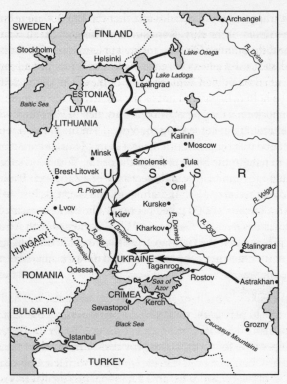

Figure 10.3 The Russian Front during 1943 and 1944.

Kursk – 'the greatest tank battle in history'

Hitler, who badly needed a victory to avenge the humiliation of Stalingrad and regain the initiative in the war, declared that the battle 'would shine like a beacon to the world,' but unfortunately he was unaware that 'Lucy', a Communist spy-ring working in Germany, had forewarned the Russians of the impending German offensive. For the battle, the Germans massed 900,000 men and 3,000 tanks, many of them formidable Panther and Tiger tanks and these were to be supported by 1,800 aircraft of the Luftwaffe. Against them, the Red Army had 1,300,000 men, 3,600 tanks, 20,000 pieces of artillery and 2,400 aircraft and, in addition, 300,000 Russian civilians worked to dig tank traps and lay minefields so that over 400,000 mines were in place in front of the Russian positions. Although Stalin wanted to move first, the cunning Zhukov insisted in letting the Germans attack first and wear themselves down against the defences he had put in place. Even though the Germans knew of the extent of the defences facing them, they launched a massive tank-led offensive against the Russian positions. In spite of heavy losses, the Germans forced the Red Army to retreat some 30 kilometres. Then the Russians counter-attacked and succeeded in destroying 40 per cent of what remained of the German tanks and within three days the German offensive had been fought to a standstill and the initiative passed to the Russians. From now on, it would be the Germans who fought defensive battles as the Red Army headed for the frontiers of Poland, Romania and the German Reich itself. The loss of life on both sides was massive with the Germans suffering up to 100,000 killed and wounded. Stalin kept details of the Soviet losses secret but following the fall of the Communist regime in 1989, they were revealed as 250,000 dead and 600,000 wounded.

After the Battle of Kursk, the Russian armies continued to advance to capture Kharkov and then reach the River Dnieper and cut off the German forces in the Crimea. Early in 1944, they reached the Black Sea port of Odessa and by the middle of July, the Red Army had crossed into Poland and were advancing towards the River Vistula. Meanwhile in the west in June, Anglo-American-Canadian forces had landed in Normandy to open the long-awaited 'second front' whilst to the south, the Allies were fighting their way through Italy.

In anticipation of imminent liberation, on 1 August 1944, Polish resistance fighters in Warsaw rose up and took on the Germans stationed in the city but the Red Army did not move to help and instead watched as the Germans ruthlessly crushed the revolt. Later some claimed that Stalin declined to assist so that the Germans could eliminate the Poles who might cause him difficulties during the post-war period. However, Soviet historians have denied this stating that the Warsaw uprising had occurred without first consulting the Russians and that after advancing 700 kilometres in five weeks, the Red Army was exhausted.

In September, the Red Army entered Romania and Bulgaria whilst further north, they swept through the Baltic States and forced the

Figure 10.4 The Russian advance into eastern Europe and the heart of Germany in 1945.

surrender of Finland. By the start of 1945, the Russians were poised to begin their final assault into the heart of Germany.

In January, the Red Army crossed the River Vistula and finally liberated Warsaw whilst elsewhere, the spearheads of the Russian advance reached deep into the Balkans to liberate Budapest and Vienna, the capitals of Hungary and Austria, and into the heart of Germany. From his bunker in Berlin, Hitler once again ordered a fight to the death as in these final stages of the war, the authorities recruited a *Volksstrum* or home guard to fight alongside the German army. In what Zhukov called their 'final hour of vengeance', the Red Army stood poised for an assault on the German capital city. Although outnumbered and outgunned, the encircled Germans fought valiantly building-by-building and street-by-street until on 30 April two Red Army sergeants, Kantariya and Yegorov, raised the Russian flag on the Reichstag building. Two days later, the city surrendered. A week earlier, Adolf Hitler, ranting and raving about the betrayal of his generals, had committed suicide in his bunker. It was not a victory easily won and again the Russian casualties were enormous. It should also be mentioned that, fuelled by a hatred of the atrocities committed by the Germans in their own country, the Russians committed appalling outrages against the civilian population with thousands of women being raped and the men who tried to intervene, shot out of hand.

On 7 May 1945, General Dwight D. Eisenhower, the Allied commander-in-chief, accepted the unconditional surrender of Germany in Rheims in France and the following day, Marshal Khukov received the German surrender in Berlin. The 8 May 1945 was celebrated as VE Day and the long, costly and bloody war in Europe was over. Across the Soviet Union there was great rejoicing and in Moscow's Red Square, people gathered to sing and dance whilst churches were packed for thanksgiving services. Stalin, now at the height of his triumphs, took the salute at a march past in Red Square and many soldiers trailed German flags and banners behind them and threw them at his feet. In a speech broadcast to the Russian people, Stalin said:

> *The war in Europe is over... I congratulate you upon victory, my dear men and women compatriots... glory to our heroic Red Army which has upheld the independence of the Motherland and won victory over the enemy... Eternal glory to the heroes who fell in the struggle and gave their lives for the freedom and happiness of our peoples.*

The Soviet Union under German occupation

The first atrocities against Russian civilians were not committed by the Germans but by the Soviet authorities themselves! As they retreated ahead of the German advance, NKVD agents shot all those they thought politically unreliable and likely to collaborate with the invaders. In the Ukraine alone, the NKVD murdered an estimated 10,000 political prisoners whilst in some areas, entire ethnic groups, the Tartars living in the Crimea and the Germans living along the River Volga, were either killed or sent in cattle wagons to Siberia.

Once the Germans had occupied the western regions of the Soviet Union, they were turned into provinces of Hitler's German empire. The Baltic Provinces became *Reichskommisariat* Osland under civilian administration whilst the Ukraine became *Reichskommisariat* Ukraine under a military administration. It was the German intention to create a state beyond the Ural Mountains for all Russians of ethnic Slav origin. Wherever racial origins allowed, the people were to 'Germanized' and when this was not possible, exterminated. In June 1941, the German High Command issued a secret document that ordered the execution of any Communist political commissars who fell into their hands, 'Action must be taken…when they are picked up, they are, as a matter of principle, to be finished immediately with a weapon.'

Hitler was determined to impose his New Order and racial policy on the Russian people. In order to do this, *Einsatzgruppen*, Special Task Forces, and *Ordnungspolizei*, the Order Police, were sent into the country to deal with the ordinary Russian Slav people who were said to be *Untermensch*, sub-human, and Russia's 2,100,000 Jews. *Einsatzkommandos*, mobile killing groups, operated across the country committing the most appalling atrocities as they set about murdering all those considered to be undesirables – Communists, particularly political commissars, and those of inferior race – Slavs and Jews. This merciless system of ethnic cleansing embraced men, women and children and was carried out by shooting them openly or by sending them to mobile gassing installations described as 'slaughter houses on wheels'. In the first months of the German occupation, 229,000 Jews were murdered in the Baltic States but the worst single atrocity occurred at Babi Yar near Kiev where in a two-day orgy of murder, an estimated 34,000 Jews were executed. In this, the Germans were helped in their work by Ukrainian collaborators. In 1942, the *Einsatzgruppen* massacred 2,892 men, women and children at Kortelisy in the Ukraine and razed their village to the ground. It was claimed that they had been helping local partisans.

During the years of German occupation, a total of over one and a half million Russian Jews perished – 71 per cent of the country's pre-war Jewish population. In 1942, Ilya Ehrenburg, a Soviet writer of

Ukrainian-Jewish origins, vented his spleen on the German race when he wrote:

> **Now we understand the Germans are not human. Now the word German has become the most terrible curse. Let us not speak. Let us not be indignant. Let us kill. If you do not kill a German, a German will kill you. He will carry away your family and torture them in his damned country. If you have killed one German, kill another.**
>
> From an article by Ilya Ehrenburg that appeared in the newspaper *Krasnaya Zvezda* in 1942

To these must be added the Russian prisoners-of-war who were sent to Germany to work as slave labour. Of these, an estimated 3 million died of ill treatment, overwork and starvation in labour camps. Within German-occupied Russia, civilians were also employed as slave labour and SS chief Heinrich Himmler summed up the Nazi view when he said, 'If ten thousand Russian families die of exhaustion digging an anti-tank trench, that interests me only in as far as the trench was dug for Germany.'

In his book *Dynamo: Defending the Honour of Kiev*, Andy Dougan tells the incredible story of the bravery of Dynamo Kiev football team. The members of the team who survived were made to work as slave labour in a bakery. In order to prove Hitler's theory of Aryan racial supremacy, these badly treated and underfed men were forced to play a match against a team of Russian collaborators and Germans and were warned beforehand that they were to lose. In spite of the fact that the referee was an SS fanatic, the Dynamo players won! On their return to the bakery, they were arrested and sent to a death camp. Later, after the war, a monument was raised in their honour.

...of collaboration and resistance

As we have seen, when the Germans first invaded the Soviet Union, in some regions they were welcomed as liberators from Stalinist oppression. This was particularly true of the Baltic States, Byelorussia and the Ukraine. Ukrainians, who still had bitter memories of Stalin's enforced starvation, even greeted the invaders with the traditional gifts of bread and salt! It was soon quite obvious that given the chance, thousands would be prepared to collaborate and even serve in the German army. Volunteers were recruited into the *Hilfswillige* and were used as labourers or to carry supplies to front line troops. A number of Ukrainians agreed to form a fighting unit within the *Waffen-SS* known as the Galacia Division. Their leader was Andrey Vlasov, a former Communist who had served with distinction in the defence of both Kiev and Moscow and had become a Hero of the Soviet Union and been awarded the Order of the Red Banner. However, taken prisoner during the siege of Leningrad, he blamed Stalin for the disaster that had befallen him and together with other Red Army deserters, formed the Russian Liberation Movement. His declared aim was 'to fight as Germany's ally for a socialist Russia and rid the country of Stalin's system of terror'. 'Vlasov's army', as his Movement became known, grew to number 50,000 men and towards the end of the war was allowed to fight in the front line against their former Red Army comrades. Eventually over a million Russians swore oaths of loyalty to Hitler and enlisted in the German army. Although most German generals accepted such volunteers with enthusiasm, Hitler was opposed to the idea of sub-human Slavs fighting alongside Aryan Germans and as a result most were given only menial tasks and became disillusioned.

In July 1941, the Central Committee of the Communist Party called upon all Russian citizens to take up arms against the Germans and as a result thousands of Russians joined the ranks of the partisan resistance fighters and continued to fight from behind the German lines. They used guerrilla tactics to harass the enemy and attacked their railways and lines of communication. They became more effective as they became better organized and were helped by officers and arms supplied by the Red Army. From time to time there were major uprisings and the Germans were forced to undertake extensive anti-partisan sweeps across the country. Those captured were hanged and there were instances when partisan activity led to the Germans taking reprisals when villages were burned to the ground and their inhabitants slaughtered.

The Soviet war economy

At the start of the war, Hitler imagined that the sudden invasion of the Soviet Union would result in all the industries in western Russia falling within his grasp and it was true that by the end of 1941, 63 per cent of the country's coal production, 68 per cent of her iron,

58 per cent of her steel lay in territory occupied by the Germans. However, much of the industrial development that took place during the Five-Year Plans was to the east of the Urals and well away from the Nazi onslaught and *blitzkrieg*. On the first day of the war, the Supreme Soviet issued a decree 'On the Military Situation', which made plans for the total mobilization of the nation's resources for the war effort. People's Commissariats were set up to supervise the various sections of war production such as tanks, guns and aircraft. Additional labour was recruited by calling on the entire urban population to undertake work in armaments' factories, including all men aged 16 to 55 and women aged 16 to 45. Office workers were transferred to munitions production and pensioners and students urged to contribute at least some part-time work.

The most remarkable achievement was the evacuation of factories in the path of the Germans and their reconstruction in the east. This involved massive operations but the Russian people, aware that the Red Army was involved in a fight to the death, were determined to provide their soldiers with adequate weapons and ammunition. Between July and November 1941, in spite of enemy air attacks intended to disrupt the operation, the transfer of 1,303 industrial units was completed. During 1942, the Russian military expenditure had reached enormous proportions with the military share of the budget rising from 29 per cent to 57 per cent and munitions accounting for 76 per cent of all production. A shortage of labour was a major problem faced by the Russian authorities and large numbers of women were recruited for factory work. Once they had mastered the required skills, they replaced men who were urgently

Table 10.1   Soviet military production 1940–44

	1940	1941	1942	1943	1944
Ammunition (millions)	63	180	238	229	109
Artillery ('000s)	30	127	130	122	72
Tanks ('000s)	4	24	24	29	20
Aircraft ('000s)	8	21	29	33	19

Source: *Years of Russia and the USSR, 1951–1991*, David Evans and Jane Jenkins, Hodder & Stoughton, 2001

needed as soldiers at the front. During this time Russian engineers designed the T34, KV-2 and JS-2 tanks, the Katyusha rocket launcher and the Yak-1 fighter aircraft, all of which were soon to be recognized as amongst the best weaponry produced by any nation during the war.

The importance of foreign aid

During the course of the war, the Soviet Union sought and received military aid from her partners in what was now called the Grand Alliance. Ships of the Royal Navy and merchant fleet ran a gauntlet as they risked German submarine and air attack as they carried their cargoes across the icy waters of the Arctic Ocean to the port of Murmansk. In all, the Arctic convoys suffered the loss of 90 ships and the lives of 829 British merchant seamen. Other aid from Britain and the United States reached Russia overland by way of Iran. By the terms of the Lend-Lease Act of 1941, the American Senate approved the sending of war materials to nations 'whose defence was considered vital to the defence of the United States'. As a result, the USA supplied the USSR with 6,430 planes, 3,734 tanks and 210,000 vehicles as well as other essential materials, food and $11 billion in financial aid. Stalin never acknowledged this generosity, so the Russian people were unaware that the help they were receiving came from capitalist countries. Instead, he criticized Britain and the United States for being slow to open a 'second front' in western Europe and ignored the fact that his allies were engaged in campaigns in North Africa and Italy as well as fighting a war against the Japanese in which Russia was not involved.

The Soviet Union's contribution to the final Allied victory

It should be remembered that in September 1939, the Soviet Union entered into an alliance with Germany and then took part in the invasion of Poland and an attack on Finland. Again, the Soviet Union did not willingly engage in a war with Germany until the country fell victim to Nazi aggression in June 1941. Soviet historians might argue that the reason for the German Soviet Treaty was Stalin's concern over the Anglo-French failure to stand up to Hitler at Munich in 1938 and the Pact was his way of buying time to prepare for a war that was inevitable. However, once involved in the war, there can be no doubt that the sacrifices made by the Russian people were enormous.

During the war, the Red Army bore the brunt of the land fighting in Europe and sustained huge losses. Britain and the United States also suffered a considerable loss of life but the numbers were only slight when compared with the Soviet Union. The British people were subjected to heavy bombing and suffered shortages whereas the United States homeland survived unscathed. In Russia, however, large tracts of land were occupied by the Germans, and the Russian people were subjected to great brutality.

In addition, much of Russia lay devastated. Oil wells and power stations were wrecked and roads and railways left impassable with some 64,000 kilometres of railway track destroyed. In the countryside, 100,000 collective farms had been laid waste and millions of cattle slain. Worst of all was the destruction of houses that left 25 million people homeless. The Germans had also looted the country's colleges, libraries, art galleries, hospitals and public buildings.

The survival of the USSR can be attributed to numerous factors – the bravery of the Russian people, the fighting qualities and ferocity of Red Army soldiers, the quality of the leadership of such men as

Table 10.2   Table 10.2 The human cost of the Second World War

	Military dead	Civilian dead
Britain	264,443	92,673
United States	229,131	6,000
*Soviet Union	11,000,000	7,000,000
Germany	3,500,000	780,000

* The figures relating to the Soviet Union are only estimates since the exact numbers will never be known. The civilian dead includes the Russian Jews murdered during the years of German occupation.

Ivan Konev, Konstantin Rossokovsky, Konstantin Timoshenko, and particularly the military genius of Marshal Zhukov. Described by the Allied commander-in-chief, Dwight D. Eisenhower, as 'a man of courage, vision, fortitude and determination,' Zhukov was arguably the greatest general of the Second World War. Much must also be attributed to the leadership of Josif Stalin who, taking the title 'Generalissimo' and describing the conflict as a 'Great Patriotic War', was largely responsible for mobilizing the country and constantly urging the Russian people to even greater effort. Wisely, in 1943 Stalin announced his recognition of the Russian Orthodox Church, a gesture much appreciated by the millions of Russians who had been forced to worship in secret. Unlike Hitler, he was prepared to listen to the advice of his generals but always made the final decision. The Russian success was also a result of major errors of judgement by Hitler, particularly at Stalingrad and Kursk, and the failure of the Germans to cope with the extremities of the Russian winter.

There is no doubt that the hard won Battle of Stalingrad marked a turning point, not merely on the Russian Front, but in the war generally. No other battle was fought with such ferocity or resulted in so many casualties. After the formation of the 'Grand Alliance' embracing Britain, the Soviet Union and the United States, relations between the three powers remained strained. However, Stalin achieved a far better working relationship with the American president, Franklin D. Roosevelt than he did with the British prime minister, Winston Churchill. Even though Stalin dissolved Comintern in 1943, the Western powers remained concerned at his long-term intentions. For his part, Stalin repeatedly urged Roosevelt and Churchill to open a second front in the West and secretly feared that their reluctance was an indication that they were content to see Germany and the Soviet Union fight themselves to a standstill. He even feared that his allies might make a separate peace with Germany and leave Russia to fight on alone!

The caption to this German cartoon of early 1944 reads 'Little Winston's fear of the water' and shows a reluctant Churchill being pushed by Stalin towards 'invasion', the opening of a Second Front in the West.

After the war, Soviet historians played down the part played by Britain and France claiming that the campaigns fought by the two allies in North Africa and Italy were unimportant sideshows and no mention was made of their ongoing war against Japan. Such historians might have reminded the Russian people that during 1940 and most of 1941, Britain stood alone against Germany and fought on when the odds were very much against her survival and that the United States made a massive financial contribution towards winning the war both against Germany and Japan.

11

Soviet foreign policy after 1945 – the Cold War

This chapter will cover:
- *the wartime and post-war conferences*
- *the division of Germany and Soviet territorial gains*
- *the collapse of the wartime alliance*
- *the imposition of Communist rule over Eastern Europe*
- *the Truman Doctrine and the Marshall Plan*
- *Berlin and other crises in East-West relations*
- *the Soviet Union, a nuclear power*
- *the Korean War.*

> *I firmly believed that after victory everything would suddenly change...it is clear that everyone expected that once victory had been won, people would know real happiness.*
>
> From *People, Years, Life* by Ilya Ehrenburg, 1960

Peace and the origins of the Cold War

As we have seen, the Grand Alliance of Britain, the Soviet Union and the United States was always uneasy and full of mistrust. During the war, a number of conferences had taken place between the leaders of the Allied powers and the first three of these, held in Placentia Bay, Newfoundland in 1941, Casablanca and Quebec in 1942, only involved Winston Churchill and Franklin D. Roosevelt. The first of these meetings produced the Atlantic Charter that asserted the right of people to choose their own form of government and live free from fear and want. The Soviet Union subsequently endorsed the Charter.

The meetings at Casablanca and Quebec were more concerned with the future conduct of the war whilst Churchill, Roosevelt and the Chinese leader, Chiang Kai-shek, attended a meeting held in Cairo late in 1943 that was largely concerned with the future of the war against Japan. The first conference attended by Stalin was held in Teheran late in 1943 and there the leaders of the three major powers came face to face. The main issues discussed included the opening of a 'second front' against Germany and the possibility of the Soviet Union entering the war against Japan. Afterwards, the omens for a good relationship based on mutual understanding seemed promising as was evident in their final declaration:

> *We express our determination that our nations shall work together in war and in the peace that will follow... We have reached complete agreement as to the scope and timing of operations to be undertaken from the east, west and south. Emerging from these cordial conferences we look forward to the day when all peoples of the world may live free lives, untouched by tyranny, and according to the varying desires and their own consciences. We came here with hope and determination. We leave here, friends in fact, in spirit and in purpose.*

Far more important were the next two meetings held at Yalta and Potsdam towards the end and just after the war, attended by those now referred to as the 'Big Three'.

The Yalta and Potsdam conferences, 1945

In February 1945, with the war still in progress, Stalin, Roosevelt and Churchill met at Yalta in the Crimea. The timing of the conference was particularly unfortunate from the viewpoint of Britain and the United States since at the time their forces were struggling to hold a German offensive in the Ardennes – the Battle of the Bulge – whilst the Russians were advancing rapidly through Poland. This gave Stalin some edge over the Western Allies that he was not slow to exploit. There they confirmed that the war would continue until Germany surrendered unconditionally and plans were made for the post-war division of Germany into four zones of occupation – British, American, Russian and French – under a control commission based in Berlin. Stalin wanted France to be excluded from the agreement and it was largely on the insistence of Churchill the country was treated as an equal partner. The future of the liberated countries was discussed and it was agreed and accepted by Stalin that at the earliest opportunity, such countries would 'establish through free elections...governments responsible to the will of the people'. Far more difficult was reaching agreement about the future of the Soviet Union's immediate neighbour, Poland. During the course of the war, two Polish governments in exile had existed, one backed by the Russians based in Lublin in Soviet liberated Poland; the other, led by Wladyslaw Sirkorski, was based in London and supported by the Western Allies. It was eventually agreed that the two would be brought together and organized on a 'broader, democratic basis' but no agreement was reached on Poland's future borders with the Soviet Union. Stalin insisted that once the war was over, all Russian prisoners-of-war liberated by Anglo-American forces should be returned to the Soviet Union without delay and, as we shall see, this decision was to have tragic consequences. The Russian leader agreed to enter the war against Japan within three months of Germany's surrender and, in return, he was offered certain territorial gains – the Kurile Islands, South Sakhalin, a zone of occupation in Korea, and Port Arthur lost to the Japanese following the Russo-Japanese War of 1904–5. The three leaders agreed to support the setting up of a United Nations Organization and to this end, a meeting of delegates from the 50 nations currently at war with Germany was called at San Francisco on 25 April. Stalin wanted all 16 Russian republics to be admitted as full members but after an agreement was reached on voting rights, the number was finally set at two – the Ukraine and Byelorussia (Belarus).

Yalta proved a great diplomatic success for Stalin since he obtained a great deal and conceded little. A feature of the conference was the differing attitudes to Stalin taken by Roosevelt and Churchill. As the American President seemed to grow more convinced of Stalin's good intentions, so the British Prime Minister became even more cautious and distrusting of the Soviet leader. Roosevelt's trust of Stalin was to have dire consequences for the future of post-war Europe and he was later accused of playing into the Russian leader's hands by agreeing to terms that would allow much of Eastern Europe to fall under Communist domination. However, in one respect Stalin did keep his promise when, six weeks before the country's surrender, he declared war on Japan. Even so, it might be argued that he only did so in order to have a say in the peace settlement in the Far East. The war was barely over when the 'Big Three' gathered for a conference in a suburb of Berlin, Potsdam.

Of the leaders who had met earlier at Yalta, now only Stalin remained. In the United States, Roosevelt had died and been replaced as president by Harry S. Truman; in Britain, the Conservatives had lost the first post-war elections and Churchill had been replaced by the leader of the new Labour Government, Clement Attlee. This meant that Stalin, the 'wily old Bolshevik' was now dealing with two relatively inexperienced new boys. After their first meeting, Truman said of the Soviet leader, 'I think I can do business with Stalin... He's very honest but he's also as smart as hell.' As previously agreed at Yalta, Germany was divided into four zones of occupation and Berlin, in the Soviet zone, was split into four sectors.

In a similar way, Austria was also to be divided between the four major powers and Vienna split into sectors. All matters affecting Germany and Austria were to be dealt with by an Allied Control Council and its policies based on what became known as the 'five Ds' – demilitarization, denazification, democratization, decentralization and deindustrialization. Since most German industry was located in the Western zones, the issue of reparations was to prove particularly difficult and, in the end, it was decided that each power had to claim reparations from its own occupied zone. In addition, the Soviet Union would receive an additional 10–15 per cent of industrial plant and machinery from the Western zones in exchange for agricultural produce from its own zone. The frontiers of Poland were again discussed and here there was considerable disagreement but, in the end, Britain and the United States agreed to drop their support for Sikorski's London-based Poles if the Russians were willing to guarantee free elections in Poland after the war. Stalin accepted this but he was not prepared to have the elections supervised by independent observers! It was eventually agreed that the Soviet Union should be allowed to retain all the land taken as a result of her invasion of Poland in 1939. Poland would be compensated at the expense of Germany by moving her frontiers westward to the banks of the Rivers Oder and Neisse.

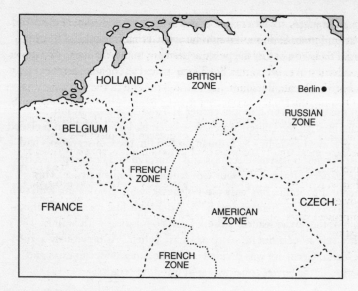

Figure 11.1 The division of Germany into four zones.

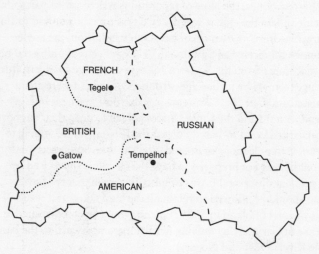

Figure 11.2 The post-war division of Germany and Berlin. In view of subsequent events, the location of airports Tegel, Gatow and Templehof were soon to have great significance.

These changes, together with others affecting Czechoslovakia and Hungary, meant that millions of ethnic Germans would be forced to leave their homes and live within Germany's new frontiers. Whatever goodwill still existed after Yalta evaporated at Potsdam and, in many ways, the Potsdam Conference marked the end of the wartime alliance of Britain, the United States and Russia. Peace settlements made with the other defeated nations – Italy, Hungary, Bulgaria, Romania and Finland – were lengthy and often involved bitter disputes. It also became increasingly clear that Stalin would not permit any outside interference in the affairs of the countries liberated by the Red Army that were now effectively under Communist control and brought Soviet influence into the very heart of Europe. Matters were not improved when President Truman informed Stalin of the successful testing of the first atomic bomb in New Mexico and of his intention to use the new weapon against Japan. This provided the United States

Figure 11.3 The frontiers of the new Poland agreed at the Potsdam Conference.

with an ace that Stalin would not be able to counter until Soviet scientists had developed their own atomic weapons. In the meantime, Truman steadfastly refused to share American nuclear secrets with the Russians and it also became increasingly clear that the Soviet Union could expect to receive little of the reparations from the Western zones of Germany promised at Potsdam. As the American historian, Walter LaFeber commented, 'Potsdam marks the point at which Truman and Stalin do not have a lot to say to one another anymore.' With diplomacy exhausted, both sides returned to promoting their rival ideologies of capitalism and communism.

The Nuremberg trials

Across occupied Germany, former leading members of the Nazi Party were arrested and brought for trial at Nuremberg to answer for their various crimes – war crimes, crimes against peace and crimes against humanity whilst across occupied Germany. Other courts dealt with thousands of other cases involving Nazi war criminals. Each of the four countries, Britain, France, the United States and the Soviet Union, provided one judge and an alternative. The Russian judge was Iola Nikitchenko who had earlier been involved in the Moscow show trials in 1936, and his alternative, Alexander Volchkov. At a meeting held before the trials began, Nikitchenko put forward his views:

> *We are dealing here with the chief war criminals who have already been convicted and whose conviction has already been announced by both the Moscow and Yalta declarations of the Allied governments... The whole idea is to secure quick and just punishment for the crime... The fact that the Nazi leaders are criminals has already been established. The task of the tribunal is only to determine the measure of guilt of each particular person and mete out the necessary punishment...*

With innumerable witnesses and masses of documentary evidence to be considered, the trials lasted for the best part of a year and at the end 12 were sentenced to death, three given life sentences, four given lesser sentences and three acquitted. Nikitchenko did not agree with some of the lesser sentences and turned down a French proposal that the German military sentenced to death should be shot and not hanged. 'They are common criminals,' Nikitchenko protested, 'who have disgraced their military ethos and tradition.'

Soviet expansion in Eastern Europe

In Eastern Europe, Stalin failed to keep his promise made at Potsdam that he would allow free elections in the countries liberated by the Red Army. It became increasingly obvious that his real intention was to impose communist rule on those countries and turn them into Soviet satellites. He achieved the expansion of Russian influence by several means – diplomatic pressure, subversion, infiltration, and offers of economic aid but, if these failed, by threats and intimidation. Of course, in countries liberated and occupied by Soviet forces, it was all too easy for Stalin to establish sympathetic regimes.

In Poland, the communists faced opposition from the rival London-based government in exile whose leader, Sikorski, was killed in an air crash off Gibraltar. The death of Sikorski was a major setback

Figure 11.4 The Soviet domination of Eastern Europe.

for the Polish cause and was most convenient for Stalin. There have been persistent suggestions that his death was not accidental and even that Winston Churchill was involved in a plot to assassinate him. His successor, Stanislaw Mikolajczyk, was politically well to the left of his colleagues and he hoped that he would be able to reach an understanding with the Russian-backed Lublin government. For a time, representatives of both former governments-in-exile merged to form a coalition, the Polish Provisional Government of National Unity, but it was an uneasy alliance. Since the Russians were in effective control of the country and the new President, Boleslaw Bierut, was a hard line Stalinist, the Communists were able to secure control of the key positions in the government and arrest representatives of the former London-based Polish government in exile on their arrival in Warsaw. Gradually Mikolajczyk lost what little influence he had and the country fell under the control of the Polish Workers' Party.

For obvious reasons, it was easy for the Communists to gain immediate control of the Russian occupied zone of Germany. The regime was forced to hand over to the Russians reparations in the form of vast quantities of machinery and equipment whilst thousands of East Germans were pressed into forced labour. Immediately after the war, Eduard Benes, Czechoslovakia's pre-war head of state, returned to his homeland and tried to hold free elections and establish democratic government. The Czechs, who were still bitter over what they considered an Anglo-French betrayal in 1938, elected a broad-based coalition government made up of left-wing parties. However, the Communists, who won 38 per cent of the vote, dominated Czech politics and this remained the situation until 1948. In Romania, King Michael first had to accept a Communist Democratic Front government until he was forced to abdicate in 1946 when the country became a People's Republic under Nicolae Ceausescu. Similarly, after King Boris was removed in Bulgaria, a predominantly Communist regime established a new republic under Georgi Dimitrov.

When the Red Army first crossed into Hungary in September 1944, they set up a provisional government in the town of Debrecen. The following year, the new Hungarian Republic held free elections in which the people voted the non-communist Smallholders' Party a majority. The Soviet Union soon found means of discrediting

the Party and replaced it with the United Workers' Party led by
Matyas Rakosi. In Albania, Enver Hoxha, who had fought with the
resistance and was now the leader of the Workers' Party established
one of the most severe communist regimes in Eastern Europe which
remained so even after Stalin's death. However, Yugoslavia was to
provide a stumbling block to Stalin's ambitions. There the popular
wartime leader, Marshal Tito, was elected president and although
a communist, he was not prepared to surrender his country's
independence and toe the Moscow line. As we shall see, this was
to bring him into direct conflict with Stalin. Another country that
frustrated Stalin's plans was Greece.

The Greek civil war

Throughout the war, two rival Greek resistance groups had fought
the Germans. One, the communist-led National Liberation Front
(EAM) backed by the National People's Liberation Army (ELAS) was
led by Aris Veloukhiotis; the other, the Greek Democratic National
League (EDES) led by Napoleon Zervas, was strongly nationalist and
republican. Neither group was prepared to support the exiled Greek
king, George II. Even before the war was over, the rival guerilla armies
had started to fight each other and if necessary betray each other to
the enemy. When the Germans withdrew from Greece in October
1944, a government in exile led by George Papandreou returned to
Athens accompanied by units of the British army. He set up a Greek
Government of National Unity but it failed to survive and the country
lapsed into open civil war until 1945 when the Communists asked for
a truce and surrendered their arms. Boycotted by left-wing parties,
the elections of 1946 returned a pro-monarchist Populist Party led
by Constantine Tsaldaris and in a referendum held on the future
of the monarchy, 70 per cent voted for the return of King George.
Meanwhile, the civil war flared up again and the British government
had to further bolster Tsaldaris with military and economic aid in
order to ensure that the communists were denied victory. Later, as
Britain found it impossible to carry the burden alone, the arrival of
American financial aid helped the Greek economy to recover and as a
degree of prosperity returned, so Greek government forces gained the
upper hand and brought the civil war to an end.

The attempted communist take-over of Greece was the first major showdown between the Western powers and the Soviet Union. Whilst Stalin would have been disappointed that the advance of communism had been halted, he would have been delighted with the growth of large and well-organized communist parties in France and Italy. At times it seemed possible that in both countries the Communists might gain power by democratic means.

The start of the Cold War

As we have seen, in Europe suspicion and uncertainty had begun to sour international relations. Although the United Nations Organization had been set up in 1945 to settle disputes and lessen international tension, nations once again began to consider forming protective alliances rather than make plans for a lasting peace. In such an atmosphere, it was always possible that confrontations might develop that could lead to crises or even worse, war, but fortunately when crises did arise, they led only to heated exchanges of words and threats. The term Cold War came into use to describe the hostile relations between the West and the Soviet Union that fell short of armed conflict – a Hot War.

Russian domination and the creation of communist regimes in Eastern Europe meant that in Western Europe there was a fear of further Soviet expansion and consequently these nations looked increasingly to the United States for security. It was known that whilst Britain and the United States had allowed a speedy demobilization, Russia still maintained her armed forces at full strength. Still, atomic weapons gave the West a decisive advantage and the United States continued to firmly refuse to share knowledge of these weapons with Russia. In the spring of 1946, Winston Churchill visited the United States and in a speech at Fulton, Missouri, the hometown of President Truman said:

From Stettin in the Baltic to Trieste in the Adriatic, an iron curtain has descended across the continent. Behind that line lie all the capitals of the states of central and eastern Europe – all are subject in one form or another not only to Soviet influence but to a very high and increasing measure of control from Moscow.

From Moscow, Stalin responded to Churchill's 'Iron Curtain' speech in the strongest possible terms:

> *Mr Churchill now takes the stand of the warmongers, and in this Mr Churchill is not alone. He has friends not only in Britain but in the United States of America as well... The following circumstances should not be forgotten... the Soviet Union's loss of life has been several times greater than that of Britain and the United States of America put together. Possibly in some quarters an inclination is felt to forget about these colossal sacrifices. But the Soviet Union cannot forget them. And so what is surprising about the fact that the Soviet Union, anxious for its future safety, is trying to ensure that governments loyal in their attitude to the Soviet Union should exist in these countries? How can anyone, who has not taken leave of his senses, describe these peaceful aspirations of the Soviet Union as expansionist tendencies on the part of our state?*

Only in two East European countries did the advance of Russian influence go unchallenged – in Yugoslavia where Tito still refused to accept direction from Moscow, and in Greece.

The Truman Doctrine and the Marshall Plan

The situation in Greece had caused the American government some concern and, in March 1947, President Truman addressed both Houses of Congress in Washington and asked them to pledge $400 million in military and economic aid to help Greece and Turkey. At the same time, he declared, 'It must be the policy of the United States to support free peoples who are resisting attempted subjugation by armed minorities or outside pressure.' The Truman Doctrine, as the declaration became known, sent a clear warning to Stalin that the United States would no longer tolerate Soviet interference in the affairs of other countries.

In June 1945, in a speech made at Harvard University, George Marshall, the American Secretary of State, put forward a plan to provide substantial and immediate economic aid to assist the recovery of war torn Europe. His plan, the European Recovery Programme but better known as the Marshall Plan, offered economic aid to all

An American cartoon of March 1947 shows Stalin's reaction to the tough line taken by President Truman.

the nations of Europe. Although Winston Churchill described the plan as 'the most unsordid act in history', Stalin saw things very differently. Suspicious that it was a devious, dollar-backed scheme to loosen the communist grip on Eastern Europe, Russia refused to accept any aid and her East European satellites faithfully followed her example. Much to the annoyance of Stalin, Tito's Yugoslavia took an independent stance and accepted Marshall Aid.

Marshall Aid certainly played a major part in preventing the Kremlin policy makers from extending their influence yet further in Europe and was one of the main reasons why democracy survived in Greece. However, as we shall see, one country remained where the communists were still prepared to use assassination and intrigue to win control.

Cominform – Comintern under another name?

Stalin's reaction to the Truman Doctrine and Marshall Plan came quickly. In October 1947, following a conference held in Warsaw attended by communist delegates from major European countries including France and Italy, the Communist Information Bureau, or Cominform, was established. The aim of the Bureau was to co-ordinate the activities of all the Communist Parties in Europe and although its headquarters was in the Yugoslav capital, Belgrade, it was controlled from Moscow. Some in the West considered Cominform to be a revival of Comintern but in reality its activities amounted to little more than publishing propaganda material aimed at encouraging solidarity amongst the East European Communist states. Ironically, the first decision taken by Cominform was the expulsion of Yugoslavia from membership and the condemnation of Marshal Tito!

During the war, Tito, his real name was Josef Broz, had led the Yugoslav resistance to the German occupation. As the war came to an end, he was able to liberate Yugoslavia without the involvement of the Red Army and once the war was over, he ruthlessly eliminated his rivals to become ruler of his country. Tito refused to allow Stalin to interfere in his country's affairs and after accepting Marshall Aid, he ignored all the threats and insults hurled at him from Moscow. Although Stalin boasted, 'I will shake my little finger – and there will be no more Tito. He will fall', but this was not to be the case. Tito's form of socialism was more liberal than was usual elsewhere in the Communist world and he also took pains to remain on good terms with the West.

The fate of Czechoslovakia

You will remember that after the war Stalin gave his support to a Czechoslovak coalition government led by Eduard Benes (see page 155) but in the elections of 1946, the communists won 114 of the 300 seats and were able to dominate the coalition government now led by Klement Gottwald. Largely because of their refusal to accept Marshall Aid, public opinion had turned against the communists and Gottwald, fearing the possible outcome of the coming election, took steps to place his supporters in all the important positions in the government.

Much depended on the speed with which Benes and his foreign minister, Tomas Masaryk, could muster support but time was against them and in February 1948, Gottwald, with Soviet backing, completed a Communist coup. Shortly afterwards Masaryk died in the most suspicious circumstances and when Gottwald introduced a Soviet-style one-party political system, Benes, a broken man, resigned and died three months later. The Western powers tried to raise the question of Czechoslovakia at the United Nations but the Russian delegate vetoed the issue.

Tito's successful defiance of Stalin made the Soviet leader even more determined to stamp out the first hint of similar movements behind the Iron Curtain. By mid-1948, Europe was truly divided by an Iron Curtain that now included barbed wire and minefields and as relations between Stalin and the West deteriorated further, so Cold War hostility turned into a vitriolic exchange of accusations and threats. One point where the Russians could exert pressure on the West was Berlin where the sectors of Britain, the United States and France lay isolated and surrounded by the Russian zone.

The Berlin blockade, 1948–9

In Berlin, the speed of recovery of the Western sectors was in sharp contrast to the still battle-scarred Russian sector. The apparent differences between the achievements of capitalism and communism were the cause of some embarrassment to the Russians since Berliners living under their control could still cross to the West and make comparisons for themselves. During 1947, Stalin was angered when the three Western zones of Berlin agreed to unite for political purposes. The Russian authorities reacted by harassing Western transport passing through their zone so that vehicles, trains and barges were held up as long queues developed at checkpoints. The situation grew worse when the Western powers agreed to introduce a new common currency, the Deutsche Mark, in their sectors. As part of a tit-for-tat trial of strength, the Russians also introduced a new currency intended for use in all the sectors of the city and to combat the move, the West made their new currency available to all Berliners. This was the last straw and on 24 June in an attempt to force the Western power to withdraw permanently from the city, the Russians closed all land and water routes into Berlin.

The American commander in Berlin, General Lucius D. Clay, realized that to use the military to force the land routes into West Berlin would trigger off a major crisis and even risk war. He therefore decided to try to supply the 2 million beleaguered West Berliners by organizing an airlift into the city. During the days that lay ahead, the RAF and the USAAF began to ferry food, fuel and medical supplies along the air corridors into the city and an endless stream of aircraft landed, one every three minutes, at Gatow, Templehof and Tegel airports. A risky business was made even more dangerous when the Russians placed weather balloons in hazardous positions and Russian MIG fighters 'buzzed' the transport planes but never actually attacked them. The Russians also tried to win over West Berliners with the use of propaganda and the offer of rations to those willing to register for the purpose but less than 2 per cent of the people took up the offer! With electricity supplies cut off, the winter of 1948–9 proved very difficult and food and fuel had to be strictly rationed. Gradually, the amount of supplies brought into the city increased with a peak being reached on 16 April 1949 when 1,383 transport planes landed in West Berlin carrying over 13,400 tonnes of supplies. Even so, the crisis over Berlin continued to escalate when Stalin declared himself unwilling to enter into any further negotiations over Berlin and President Truman ordered American B-52 bombers to Britain. On 12 May 1949, the blockade was lifted.

The failure of the Berlin blockade represented a considerable moral defeat for Stalin and made the Western Allies even more mindful of the Communist threat. In 1949, without consulting the Soviet Union, the Western powers merged their zones of Germany to form the Federal Republic of Germany (FDR) under the leadership of Konrad Adenauer and with Bonn as its capital. The Russians retaliated by transforming their zone into the German Democratic Republic (DDR) under the leadership of Walter Ulbricht.

Fearing that they would be unable to withstand a Russian attack, in April 1949 the Western powers on both sides of the Atlantic signed the North Atlantic Pact that created the North Atlantic Treaty Organization (NATO). Members of NATO placed their forces under the supreme command of the American general, Dwight D. Eisenhower. The Russians bitterly denounced NATO and claimed that it was evidence that the West was making preparations for war. Earlier in 1949, the Soviet Union had set up the Council for Mutual Economic Assistance (COMECON) with its headquarters in Moscow. It was to arrange bilateral trade agreements and was successful in establishing a common railway network and electricity grid across Eastern Europe. In 1955, two years after Stalin's death, the Russians established a military rival to NATO, the Warsaw Pact. The Pact allowed Russian troops to be stationed in Communist-bloc countries and placed their armies jointly under the command of a Russian general.

The Soviet Union becomes a nuclear power

Although at Potsdam in 1945 Stalin hid his concern and congratulated Truman on his country's development of 'a new weapon of unusual destructive force', behind the scenes Soviet scientists had been conducting their own research into atomic weapons since 1940. Later the Soviet leader expressed his true feelings when he said to Molotov, 'Let them. We'll have to talk it over with Kurchatov and get him to speed things up.' Yuri Kurchatov, the country's leading atomic scientist, was soon to be dubbed 'the father of the Soviet atomic bomb'. Back in Moscow, Stalin spoke to a gathering of atomic scientists, 'A single demand of you comrades. Provide us with atomic weapons in the shortest possible time…it will remove a great danger to us.' With unlimited funds made available and an army of scientists and technicians at his disposal, Kurchatov worked tirelessly and on 22 September 1949, the first Russian atomic bomb was successfully tested at a site in Kazakhstan. The rapid progress made by Russian scientists was helped by the treachery of a number of Western scientists.

The atom spies

Of those who supplied the Russians with secret information, Klaus Fuchs made the greatest contribution. A German by birth, Fuchs fled from Nazi Germany in the 1930s, took British nationality and was sent to the United States where he worked on the Manhattan Project at Los Alamos. During this time he secretly passed a great deal of information to the Russians and after his arrest in 1950, confessed to his betrayal. Another British scientist, Allan Nun May, was part of a Soviet spy ring based in Canada and he too pleaded guilty once his treachery was exposed. The Italian-born scientist Bruno Pontecovo emigrated to the United States and whilst working on atomic projects passed important information to the Russians. At the point of being discovered, he managed to avoid arrest and escaped to the Soviet Union. Americans who spied for the Russians included Harry Gold, the husband and wife Julius and Ethel Rosenberg, David Greenglass, Morton Sobell, William Perl and Elizabeth Bentley. Although most of the information he passed was fantasy, Gold, son of poor Jewish immigrants to the United States, was sentenced to 30 years imprisonment. The Rosenbergs, found guilty of spying for Russia, were sentenced to death and in a final emotional letter to their children, they wrote, 'Always remember that we were innocent and could not wrong our consciences.' Some hold the view that the Rosenbergs were unfortunate victims of Cold War hysteria. Greenglass, brother of Ethel Rosenberg, saved his skin by giving evidence against his sister and her husband, whilst Perl, also associated with the Rosenbergs, served a term of imprisonment. Bentley, a former fascist who changed her mind and joined the American Communist Party, provided the American FBI with information about numerous traitors and spies. Much of her testimony was untrue and, nicknamed the 'Red Spy Queen', she later became something of a celebrity. Such is the world of espionage that some of the traitors were themselves betrayed by a Soviet embassy official in Canada, Igor Gouzenko, who defected and worked for the West! For the most part, those who spied for Russia did so for ideological reasons and not for money. Fuchs claimed that his crime could not be treason since the Soviet Union was not an enemy whilst May said, 'I gave and had given very careful consideration to the correctness of making sure that the development of atomic energy was not confined to the USA.' Was it naïve of them to believe that the world would be a safer place if atomic secrets were shared amongst all the major powers? Anyway, recent revelations indicate that most of the information passed by the atom spies was already known to Soviet scientists. Greater damage was probably done by the betrayal of the so-called 'Cambridge Apostles', the British diplomats Guy Burgess, Donald MacLean and later Kim Philby, when they passed sensitive political information and then fled to the Soviet Union. Another member of the group, Anthony Blunt, became Surveyor of the Queen's Pictures until he was disgraced when details of his past were revealed in 1979.

The West's efforts to contain the spread of communism were not limited to Europe. In China, the success of the Communists in

1949 provided the Soviet Union not only with a powerful ally but a dangerous rival for the leadership of the communist world. In the Far East, the communists became active in other countries particularly colonial territories recently liberated from the Japanese. For six years the British fought elusive communist terrorists in the Malay jungle whilst in Indo-China, the communist-backed Viet Minh opposed the French as they struggled to regain control of their former colony. By far the most serious crisis occurred in 1950 in Korea.

The Soviet Union and the Korean War

After the war, the Korean peninsula was divided into the Soviet sponsored People's Democratic Republic of North Korea and to the south, the American-backed Republic of Korea. A proposal that all-Korean elections should be held in order to unify the country was turned down by the Soviet Union. On 25 June 1950, the North Koreans took matters into their own hands, crossed the demarcation line along the 38th parallel and invaded the South. At the United Nations, the United States condemned the aggression and put before the Security Council a resolution calling for an international force to be sent to the south to help repel the invaders. At the time, the Russians were boycotting Security Council meetings in protest against the UN's refusal to offer Communist China a seat on the Council and consequently the Soviet delegate to the UN, Jacob Malik, was absent from the meeting and failed to record a Russian veto.

Altogether 15 nations contributed troops to the UN force sent to South Korea and they were placed under the command of the famous American Second World War general, Douglas MacArthur. When UN forces advanced towards the Yalu River, some 200,000 Chinese 'volunteers' – they were really regular units of the Chinese army – joined the North Koreans. As the UN forces were forced to retreat, MacArthur asked for permission to use atomic weapons but President Truman refused to sanction this and dismissed the general. Ceasefire talks began in July 1951 but an armistice was not agreed until July 1953, three months after Stalin's death. The passing of the Soviet leader did bring some relaxation in East–West relations but the Cold War was far from over.

12

....

The final years of Stalin's rule

This chapter will cover:
- *the reconstruction of post-war Russia*
- *the return to Stalinist tyranny*
- *Zhdanovism and Russian culture*
- *anti-Semitism and the 'Doctors' Plot'*
- *the death of Stalin*.

When Stalin said dance, a wise man danced.

A comment by Khrushchev in 1951

Introduction

By the end of the war in Europe, the prestige of the Soviet Union and Stalin could not have been higher. The Soviet leader, who played down the roles of his generals and accepted the lion's share of the credit, delighted in the adulation of the Russian people. He made only limited references to the achievements of the Red Army or the important role played by the workers and ignored totally the contribution made by the Soviet Union's wartime allies. Once again, every form of propaganda was used to promote Stalin's image as his cult of personality reached new dimensions and approached deification. At this stage, the Second World War was not yet over since the conflict with Japan still had to be won. On 6 August 1945, the Americans dropped the first atomic bomb on the Japanese city of Hiroshima and two days later the Soviet Union declared war on Japan. The following day a second bomb was dropped on Nagasaki and on 15 August 1945, Japan surrendered and at last, the war was finally over.

Post-war reconstruction

Large areas of the Soviet Union that had been fought over and occupied by the Germans were left devastated with villages, towns and cities razed to the ground. With factories in ruins and mines flooded, something approaching 70 per cent of the nation's industrial production had been lost. Matters were made more difficult by the fact that many of the soldiers returning to civilian life were either physically or mentally scarred by their experiences and would never be able to work again. In 1946, Stalin announced the introduction of a Fourth Five-Year Plan aimed at national reconstruction. In spite of the shortage of skilled labour, the Russian people returned to work and showed the same enthusiasm and self-sacrifice as they had for the Five-Year Plans of the 1930s and had been evident during the war. By 1947, the hydroelectric power station on the Dnieper Dam was back in action, production in the Donetz Basin had overtaken that of 1940 and the national production of coal and steel had surpassed pre-war figures. The speed of Soviet industrial recovery created problems since it led to congestion and bottlenecks in production and shortages of essential raw materials and machine parts. Whilst there was some limited increase in the production of consumer goods, clothes, furniture and household appliances, they remained in short supply and had to be queued for. To some extent, industrial recovery was aided by the confiscation of machinery, rolling stock and other materials taken as reparations from the defeated countries whilst German prisoners-of-war and *gulag* slave labour also played an important role.

Steps taken to assist the recovery of Soviet agriculture proved less successful. The Germans had destroyed the collective farms, slaughtered livestock and much of the arable land had been left uncultivated. During the war, many peasants had once again grown used to cultivating their own plots and were less than enthusiastic about returning to collective farming. In addition, since the Red Army had been largely a peasant army and suffered a heavy loss of life, there was an acute shortage of labour. As in the 1930s, Stalin still only regarded agriculture as important as a means of feeding the urban workers, so he took steps to force the peasants back into the *kolkhozes* and restock their farms. In addition to shortages and the lack of motivation, there were also severe droughts and the grain harvest of 1946 was less than half that of 1940. Scarcity of food caused many to suffer from malnutrition and there was a fear that famine might return. The peasants also had other reasons for discontent since whilst they were put under pressure to produce more, procurements – the amount of their produce allocated to the state – were increased so that it accounted for up to 70 per cent of their harvest. Increases in taxation made it difficult for families to survive on what was left of their meagre earnings and the loss of their entitlement to food rations meant that they were expected to be self-sufficient and fend for themselves. Those who continued to work their own land had their plots confiscated whilst private trading – selling from market stalls – was forbidden.

In 1948, Stalin introduced his plan for what he called the 'transformation of nature'. This included the extensive planting of trees to prevent erosion, the building of irrigation canals and taking on board the crackpot ideas of the controversial agricultural scientist, Trofim Lysenko. Lysenko was a Ukrainian employed at an agricultural experimental station until he was appointed head of the All-Union Institute of Selection and Genetics based at Odessa. Based on crude and largely unproven experiments, he put forward the theory of vernalization, which stated that the quality of crops depended on environmental influences and not genetics. According to his theory, crops and animals could acquire new characteristics by being placed in a different environment. For an example, Lysenko claimed that grain intended for spring sowing could be changed to grain suitable for winter growing if it was subject to moistening and refrigeration. He even went as far as to suggest that wheat raised in the appropriate environment could produce grains of rye. A critic, and he had many, likened this to claiming that dogs brought up in the wild could give birth to foxes! Nevertheless, Stalin saw to it that Lysenko's theories became the controlling influence in Soviet agriculture but after the Soviet leader's death in 1953, Lysenko was openly ridiculed and removed from office.

During this period, Nikita Khrushchev, First Secretary of the Moscow Party and a rising member of the Politburo, tried to interest Stalin in his own plan to set up *agrogorods*. His idea was to amalgamate *kolkhozes* into larger units based on town-like settlements. These settlements would provide a full range of utilities – community centres, clinics, hospitals, nurseries and schools. The peasants would leave their lowly rural dwellings and move into blocks of flats equipped with electricity, water and sanitation. The scheme certainly did not appeal to the agricultural workers and at the Party Congress in 1952, Georgy Malenkov spoke out against Khrushchev's plan to introduce *agrogorods* claiming that they were a mistake and too expensive, as a consequence of this the whole idea was dropped. Soviet agriculture was to remain beset with problems that continued to defy solution.

A return to Stalinist tyranny

During the immediate post-war years, Stalin's behaviour became increasingly morose and irrational and he appeared emotionally unstable with his paranoia evident in his deep distrust and suspicion of all those around him. He made very few public appearances and lived in seclusion in his *dacha*, country house, or Black Sea residence. Few people were allowed close to him and his fear of imaginary enemies led to him having his food tasted for poison and his rooms regularly searched. If he travelled, his route was changed to thwart any assassination attempt and there was an instance when a youth was shot for daring to glance at his passing train! Friendly one day and hostile the next, Party leaders lived in fear of his mood swings, which led to people to being arrested and their disappearance. Sometimes Stalin organized parties that involved heavy drinking and crude horseplay that included ridiculing guests. Later Khrushchev commented, 'When Stalin said dance, a wise man danced.' The advancing years certainly made Stalin more malevolent and vindictive but did Stalin really undergo a personality change or were these abnormalities in his character evident in the 1930s? Whatever, the Soviet propaganda machine continued to promote their great leader and boasted of the 'solidarity of the Soviet peoples under their leader of genius, J. V. Stalin'.

Years of 'hysterical isolationism'

During the period 1945–53, Stalin took every possible measure to ensure that his people were denied access to the outside world and remained unaffected by Western influences. He claimed that the reason for this was that the country was threatened by the capitalist powers who were plotting to overthrow their communist regime. The Russian people were warned to be on their guard and denounce any 'hidden agents of Western imperialism'. Russians were not allowed to travel abroad and the few foreigners permitted to visit the Soviet Union were kept under constant surveillance. The Soviet historian, Yuri Levada, has described the years as a period of 'hysterical isolationism'. In truth these measures had nothing to do with national security but were intended to ensure that Stalin's dictatorship continued uninterrupted.

The Soviet leader was concerned that Red Army soldiers who had fought their way across eastern Europe and into Germany and prisoners-of-war returning to Russia might have become contaminated by Western influences. One returning Russian soldier is reported to have said, 'the standard of living was incomparable with the standard of living in Russia…and shops had a great many things we had long forgotten about'. Such an observation would have been considered subversive and had the direst consequences. This made it necessary for the authorities to carefully screen returning servicemen and many were arrested and sent to the *gulag* labour camps. As agreed at Potsdam, all Russian prisoners-of-war liberated by the British and Americans had to be forcibly repatriated to the Soviet Union. Even though many had suffered appallingly at the hands of the Germans and some had made their escape and fought with local resistance groups, Stalin considered all prisoners-of-war to be traitors or collaborators. Some, aware of what awaited, chose to commit suicide rather than go home! An eyewitness recalled the reception of Russian prisoners-of-war at Odessa:

The Soviet authorities refused to accept stretcher cases and even patients who were dying were made to walk off the ship carrying their own baggage… The prisoner who had attempted suicide was very roughly handled and his wound opened up and allowed to bleed. He was taken off the ship and marched behind a packing case, a shot was heard… The other 32 prisoners were marched or dragged some 50 yards from the ship into a warehouse and after a lapse of 15 minutes, automatic fire was heard. They were not the only victims. Altogether about 150 Russians were separated from the rest and marched behind the sheds on the quayside. They were massacred by executioners many of whom appeared to be youths aged between 14 and 16.

From *Victims of Yalta* by Nikolai Tolstoy, 1977

Of course, there was no forgiveness for those who had fought under Andrey Vlasov in the Russian Liberation Army. At the end of the war, Vlasov and his men had chosen to surrender to the Americans but they were handed over to the Soviet authorities and executed after a summary trial. Vlasov himself was tortured before being hanged in Lubyanka in 1946. The malicious Stalin next set out to remove every vestige of independent thought and eliminate anyone, within or outside the Party, who stood in his way or could possibly pose a threat. To ensure that outsiders could not influence his people, it became extremely risky to speak to any visitor from the West. The journalist Harrison Salisbury recalled:

> *I had many friends in Moscow, I telephoned some of them...when they heard my voice, they hung up...As I walked down Gorki Street, not infrequently I met someone whom I had met during the war. At first I tried to speak to them, but they looked right through me and walked ahead without speaking. I quickly realized it was too dangerous to talk to me...for any Russian to have contact with me was the equivalent of...a one-way ticket to Siberia.*

> From *American in Russia* by Harrison Salisbury, 1950

The tragedy was that in such an atmosphere of fear and intimidation, Russians regarded each other warily and with secret police and informers everywhere, it was possible to be arrested for a mere slip of the tongue and any hint of independent thought was considered inappropriate. Many looked for the opportunity to curry favour with the authorities by unearthing and denouncing those who expressed dissident views. Those arrested were interrogated and some tortured before invariably being found guilty and sent to the *gulags*. Life in the prison camps was harsh with long working hours and near starvation rations and although people were originally sent for a specified number of years, it was not unusual for sentences to be extended over and over again for no valid reason. One of those who experienced life in the *gulags* was the author Aleksandr Solzhenitsyn and in *One Day in the Life of Ivan Denisovich*, he describes moments in the life of a man about to be punished by being sent to the punishment cells:

> *Shukkov began to eat the cabbage in what was left of his gruel. He came across a small piece of potato...an average sort of piece, frostbitten of course, and rather hard and sweet. But there was very little fish...Your belly is a cruel master – however well you've*

treated it one day, it'll be singing for more the next. 'Well, good-bye brothers,' he said and nodded in a confused way... He followed the warder out. A few voices shouted after him:

'Keep cheerful. Don't let them get you down.' The men knew the cells, they'd built them themselves: stone walls, cement floor, no windows, a stove lit only to melt the ice on the walls... You slept on bare boards, and if your teeth did not fall out from chattering, survived on 300 grams of bread to eat a day – and gruel on every third day. Ten days in the cells meant that your health was ruined for life... Fifteen days – and you were a dead man.

From *One Day in the Life of Ivan Denisovich* by Aleksandr Solzhenitsyn, 1970

The system of terror was supervised by the secret police, the NKVD, under the leadership of the loathsome Lavrenti Beria. Beria was a Georgian who, although he had qualified as an architect, chose to serve in the secret police and in 1938 was appointed head of the NKVD. A sinister but highly intelligent man, he used his cunning to unscrupulously manipulate those around him. He came to wield immense power and was largely responsible for the development of the system of labour camps, the *gulags*. A known paedophile, he used terror to satisfy his sexual appetite and ambition. Amongst those who detested the man was Stalin's daughter, Svetlana Alliluyeva, who described him as 'a terrifying evil genius'.

Eminent national figures in all walks of life who were arrested and then simply disappeared, suffered a further indignity by having their names erased from all books and records and most especially the massive volume of Russian biography, the *Great Soviet Encyclopaedia*. Afterwards, as far as the Russian people were concerned, it was as if they had never lived.

Zhdanov's purge of Soviet culture

If freedom of thought was considered a threat to Stalin's regime then obviously those most likely to offend were the educated intelligentsia – teachers, lecturers, writers and those involved in the arts. To counter this, Andrei Zhdanov organized what amounted to a cultural purge intended to bring all the creative and expressive arts under his control and to establish guidelines to which all had to conform. You will remember that in 1934 Zhdanov had succeeded Kirov as the head of the Leningrad Party and played a leading role in the defence of the city during the Second World War. In 1947, he was also instrumental in setting up Cominform.

Zhdanovism, or *Zedanovshchina* as it was known, aimed to ensure that all artistic and intellectual activity was geared to conform to communist ideals and promote Stalinism and the cult of Stalin. It was equally important that it made sure that Western influences were rejected as being bourgeois, decadent and inferior to Soviet standards. Strict directives were issued and those who refused to accept Zhdanov's version of Socialist Realism risked having their works ignored, their careers ended and even their lives placed at risk. He began his campaign with a vicious attack on two highly regarded Leningrad writers, Anna Akhmatova and Mikhail Zoshchenko. He described Akhmatova, a poet whose husband and son had already been sent to the *gulags*, as 'half nun and half whore' and took particular exception to Zoshchenko's satirical *Adventures of a Monkey* that he claimed was 'malicious and insulting to the Russian people'. Both were expelled from the Union of Soviet Writers and their works banned. After Stalin's death they were rehabilitated and in 1965 Anna Akhmatova travelled to Britain to receive an honorary degree from Oxford University. Others to suffer under Zhdanovism were the composers Shostakovich and Prokofiev who were accused of 'following bourgeois ideology fed by the influence of West European and American music instead of using popular Russian melodies'. At first Shostakovich found the courage to stand up to Zhdanov but then gave way and admitted, 'I know the Party is right...and that I must search for creative paths which lead to Soviet realistic popular art'. The free-thinking Russian intelligentsia were ridiculed and humiliated whilst literary scholars were denounced for neglecting the works of Russian writers in favour of such as Shakespeare, Dickens, Rousseau and Molière. Zhdanov went to absurd lengths when he insisted that Soviet propagandists should claim that all Western inventions and scientific advances were really of Russian origin. This was also the time when the unconventional ideas of Trofim Lysenko (see Chapter 12) were promoted as the official Party line and scientists had to pay at least lip-service to his ludicrous ideas.

Zhdanovism created a barrier that prevented the normal exchange of ideas between Russia and the outside world and came to be regarded as a period of stagnation in Soviet artistic and cultural development. Andrei Zhdanov died suddenly in 1948 and, being a close confidante and supporter of Stalin, it has been suggested that he may have become too influential and that his death may have been at his leader's instigation!

Conspiracies and a purge of the Party

For a time, the patriotic fervour of the war years extended into the post-war period and there was a new enthusiasm for the Communist Party. Many ambitious newcomers sought to join the Party to enhance their career prospects even if it meant supporting Zhdanov's campaign against Western influences and by 1950 Party membership had risen to over 5.5 million. This new wave of young staunch supporters gave Stalin the opportunity to rid himself of those whose enthusiasm had started to wane and were no longer of much use to the Party. The purge began in Leningrad where many high-ranking Party members, including former close associates of Zhdanov, were arrested and either imprisoned or executed. Afterwards, the purge of the Party became nationwide and, similar to the 1930s, thousands of officials, many of them long-serving and loyal Party members, were arrested to face unfounded charges of conspiracy and treason. Amongst those arrested was Polina Zhemchuzhina, Molotov's Jewish wife, who was heard speaking in Hebrew to a foreign visitor. The foreign visitor was Golda Meir, the first Israeli ambassador to the Soviet Union who in 1969 became prime minister of her country! As Party leaders competed for his favour and jockeyed for position, Stalin appeared to enjoy a grotesque game of musical chairs as he played one off against the other. No one seemed safe since the apparent friendship of the leader might well prove to be temporary and end in their arrest and execution!

What were the reasons for Stalin's purge of the Party? Had he become an unbalanced psychopath or was it, as some historians have stated, further evidence of Stalin's paranoia – his suspicion of those around him particularly the rising young leaders within the Party?

Again...what was happening to Stalin's own family?

During this period, Stalin's own family was not spared and it suffered in much the same way as any other. The Germans had taken Yakov, his elder son, prisoner. A Red Army officer, they tried but failed to use him for propaganda purposes but after suffering much abuse from both his guards and his fellow prisoners, he finally took is own life and died in captivity. Back in Russia, Stalin imprisoned his deceased son's Jewish wife, Julia, whilst he sent his late wife's sisters to labour camps because, according to him, they 'talked a lot and knew too much'.

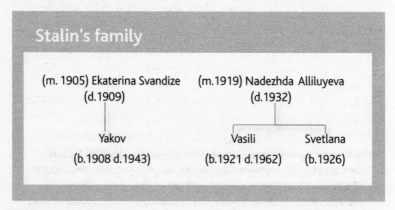

Stalin's family

(m. 1905) Ekaterina Svandize (d.1909)

Yakov (b.1908 d.1943)

(m.1919) Nadezhda Alliluyeva (d.1932)

Vasili (b.1921 d.1962)

Svetlana (b.1926)

Vasili, his younger son, became a notorious alcoholic and womanizer who served in the Red Air Force and died of cirrhosis of the liver in 1962. However, it was Svetlana, Stalin's daughter and favourite, who led the most eventful life. At 16, she first fell in love with a Jewish filmmaker, Alexej Kapler, but her father disapproved of the relationship and he was exiled in Siberia for ten years. It was claimed that he died there but subsequent research has shown that he met an actress, Valentina Tokarskaya, and they married. Later, after Stalin's death, they returned to Moscow. Next Svetlana met and married a university student, Grigori Morozov, who was also Jewish. Stalin never met his son-in-law and the marriage was short lived. Next she married Yuri Zhdanov, son of the infamous Andrei, but that too was dissolved. After her father's death, Svetlana abandoned her father's surname and took her mother's maiden name, Alliluyeva. In 1967, she defected to the United States and there denounced her father's regime and published her autobiography, *20 Letters to a Friend*. In

America, she married William Peters but again it didn't work out and in 1982, she came to Britain and made her home in Cambridge. Two years later she returned to the Soviet Union but unfortunately, her daughter failed to settle and in 1986 she returned again to the United States and now lives in a retirement home in Wisconsin. Altogether, Stalin had eight grandchildren but only three ever met their grandfather.

Stalin's seventieth birthday – the cult of personality gone berserk

In these latter years, the cult of personality that surrounded the brooding old man reached ridiculous proportions. Treated like a god, none dared to question his infallibility and in 1949, his seventieth birthday celebrations were an orchestrated mass-celebration that turned into an orgy of adulation and flattery as a massive crowd gathered in Red Square to gaze at a gigantic portrait of their leader illuminated by searchlights and suspended from a balloon. Tamara Banketik was one of those in the crowd:

> *I was transported into a fairy tale. I had eyes only for him. He had such kindly eyes. It was as if he was my father. I just wanted to touch him. We lived in terrible conditions but knew that our society was just and that capitalism was terrible and people were exploited. That is what we were taught.*

Even leaders of the Orthodox Church thanked God for giving Russia 'a pillar of social justice'. Masses of congratulatory letters and telegrams arrived from world leaders whilst across the country giant statues were erected and streets, towns and even mountains renamed in his honour. Busts of Stalin were manufactured and distributed and exhibitions organized that covered the events of his life. A rule was even introduced that specified how close people were allowed to get to Stalin when he was in a crowd! In a speech in the Bolshoi theatre in Moscow, Nikita Khrushchev, newly appointed Party leader in Moscow, said:

> *He (Stalin) has taught us the Bolshevik mode of work and sharp implacability to the slightest manifestation of alien, bourgeois nationalism, rootless cosmopolitanism and servility before decadent bourgeois culture.*

Stalinist anti-Semitism and the 'Doctors' Plot'

During the Second World War, an Anti-Fascist Jewish Committee was set up to support the war effort and thousands of Jews served in the Russian armed forces but after the war anti-Semitism once again became commonplace. In 1948, the Committee was dissolved and most of its members arrested and shot. Stalin had always shown anti-Semitic tendencies and his distrust of the Jews increased because over the years thousands of Russian Jews had emigrated to the United States and some now held positions of influence in their adopted country. It was also unacceptable to him that so many Russian Jews had relatives in the West and he was concerned that their loyalty might be more to international Jewry than to their homeland. Although the Soviet Union had been amongst the first countries to recognize the state of Israel after it had been established in 1948, Stalin recognized that the country had close ties with the West. Amongst the unfortunate Jews that remained in Russia, the authorities suspected that there might be Western agents and saboteurs. Described as 'rootless cosmopolitans' and accused of being part of an American-backed Zionist conspiracy, they were subjected to hostile propaganda and hounded by Beria's secret police. In 1953, Stalin's anti-Jewish campaign reached a climax with the unearthing of proof of a Zionist conspiracy, the 'Doctors' Plot'.

On 13 January 1953, nine doctors were arrested who had been part of a team of medical specialists responsible for the care of leading Party and government officials. All professors and established specialists in their various fields, they included Vladislav Vinogradov, Stalin's personal physician, Yakov Etinger, Alexander Grinstein, the brothers Boris and Mikhail Kogan, and Miron Vovsi. They were accused of poisoning Zhdanov and the military administrator and member of the Politburo, Alexander Shcherbakov, and of being implicated in the attempted murder of other senior officers in the Red Army. Of the nine doctors arrested, six were Jews and two, Yakov Etinger and Boris Kogan, died whilst undergoing interrogation. It was claimed that they had confessed to working for the British and American intelligence services and a banner headline in *Pravda* read, 'Vicious Spies and Killers under the Mask of Academic Physicians'. The accompanying account read:

The terrorist group...had as its goal shortening the lives of leaders of the Soviet Union by means of medical sabotage. Investigation has

*established that members of the terrorist group, exploiting their
position as doctors and abusing the trust of patients', deliberately
and viciously undermined their patients health by making incorrect
diagnoses and then killed them with incorrect treatments... The
majority of the participants of the terrorist group were bought by
American intelligence. They were recruited by the international
Jewish bourgeois nationalist organization called 'Joint'. The filthy
face of this Zionist spy organization, covering up their vicious actions
under the mask of kindness, is now completely revealed.*

The charges against the Jewish doctors were completely groundless
but, as Stalin intended, the revelations led to a backlash against
Russian Jews generally. Described as 'killers in white gowns', the
Russian people were alarmed by outlandish rumours that accused
Jewish doctors of infecting healthy people with cancer tumours.
Gossip had it that all Jewish doctors were being sent to the *gulags*
and people stopped attending their surgeries whilst ordinary Jews
were attacked in the streets, their children bruised and beaten at
school and synagogues and Jewish cemeteries desecrated. There was
also speculation that Stalin intended to deport all Russian Jews to
the remote wastes of Birobidzan. During the German occupation,
the Nazis had slaughtered over 2 million Russian Jews and it now
seemed possible that Stalin was going to complete the job and
instigate a holocaust of his own. It was also possible that Stalin's
campaign against the Jews was but a part of another purge – this time
a 'choreographed blockbuster' or 'megapurge' – of the leaders and
membership of the Communist Party and suspect Russians generally.
It did not come about since, on 5 March 1953, Josif Stalin died.

The final days and death of Josif Stalin

On the night of 1 March 1953, Stalin suffered a stroke and suffered
a part paralysis and loss of his power of speech and it appeared that
some considerable time elapsed between the nurse's discovery of him
in a collapsed state and the arrival of medical assistance. Beria was
the first to arrive on the scene and, although Stalin was clearly close
to death, he sent others away claiming that their leader was only
sleeping. The best part of a day passed before a doctor arrived and
diagnosed a stroke. Briefly, Stalin showed signs of improvement and
it is said that Beria knelt at his bedside and grovelled, forgetful of the

fact that closeness to his leader would not guarantee his survival if Stalin recovered. Svetlana arrived to witness her father's last hours:

> *There was a large crowd of people jammed into one big room where my father was lying unconscious... There was only one person who was behaving in a way that was nearly obscene. That was Beria. He was extremely agitated. His face, repulsive enough at best, now was twisted by his passions, by ambition, cruelty, cunning and a lust for power. As the end was approaching, Beria suddenly caught sight of me and ordered 'Take Svetlana away'. But no one moved... I was sitting at my father's side holding his hand and he looked at me. I kissed his face and hand. There was no longer anything more for me to do... My father died a difficult and terrible death. It was the first and so far the only time I have seen somebody die. God grants an easy death only to the just.*

From *20 Letters to a Friend* by Svetlana Alliluyeva, 1967

That morning a radio bulletin informed the Russian people that 'the life of the wise leader and leader of the Communist Party and Soviet people, Lenin's comrade and brilliant disciple, J. V. Stalin, is over'. The news led to spontaneous and widespread grief across Russia and people cried openly in the streets. It is said that some of those being held in the *gulags* even cried – one can only assume they were tears of joy! In Moscow, people came to pay homage as the body of their dead leader lay in state in the Hall of Columns. On 9 March, Malenkov, Beria, Khrushchev, Molotov, Voroshilov and his son, Vasily, carried the coffin bearing Stalin's embalmed body to its final resting place beside Lenin in the mausoleum in Red Square. Stalin left no obvious heir and as the Russian people mourned the passing of their Supreme Leader and Father of the People, so the Party hierarchy prepared for an inevitable power struggle.

By way of a postscript to these events, it must be mentioned that there is speculation amongst some historians that Stalin did not die an entirely natural death and that he may have been helped on his way. There is a view that Beria possibly poisoned him and Khrushchev later explained the delay in sending for medical assistance by stating that they thought he was suffering from a hangover. It is certainly true that Stalin's death must have come as a relief to senior Party members since they were aware that he was planning another purge which might have well involved them.

13

Stalinist Russia – a postscript

This chapter will cover:
- *the immediate aftermath of Stalin's death*
- *the impact of Khrushchev's speech at the Twentieth Party Conferennce*
- *de-Stalinization*
- *some contrasting views of Stalin.*

  The greatest criminal in history.

  Molovan Djilas's view of Stalin

Stalin's death – the aftermath

Bereft of the leadership of their beloved Stalin, the Russian people were concerned about the future of their country and there was much speculation about his successor. There was talk of a collective leadership, possibly a triumvirate comprising Party Secretary, Georgy Malenkov, the security chief, Lavrenty Beria and the former foreign secretary, Vyacheslav Molotov. Whilst they were the obvious front-runners, there were other outsiders in with a chance such as the astute Anastas Mikoyan, the Red Army general, Kliment Voroshilov, Lazar Kaganovich, the only Jew to remain a member of Stalin's inner circle, and Nikita Khrushchev. In the end, Malenkov became prime minister and Khrushchev, First Secretary of the Communist Party.

The death of Stalin immediately placed the much-hated Beria in a precarious position since the others had long been conspiring against him. In an attempt to save his skin, he suddenly claimed to be a liberal in favour of reforms, offered amnesties to many of those held in the *gulags* and admitted that those involved in the 'Doctors'

Plot' had been framed and that their confessions had been obtained by 'inadmissible methods'. His ploy failed and he was arrested and put on trial accused amongst other things of being a British agent. Although he pleaded for his life, he was shot together with six others considered to be his accomplices.

Khrushchev's speech at the Twentieth Party Conference

In 1956, at the Twentieth Party Conference, a speech made by Nikita Khrushchev to the 1,500 assembled delegates turned out to be a real bombshell. Unexpectedly he took the opportunity to reveal the stark truth about the Stalinist years and accused their former leader of flagrant abuses of power, acts of gross brutality and developing his own cult of personality. Khrushchev detailed the mass arrests of the purges, the unjustified executions and the suffering of those sent to the labour camps. He accused Stalin of the murder of Kirov and called for the rehabilitation of Trotsky. Khrushchev certainly didn't mince his words:

> *He killed thousands of Communists and ordered the mass deportations of whole nations. He was capricious, irritable and brutal, a very distrustful man, diseased with suspicion. His military ignorance cost us much blood. His rule was one of torture and oppression.*

The historian Stephen J. Lee suggests that Khrushchev may have had other motives for his denunciation:

> *After his death, Stalin's monolith threatened to leave his successors in the shade, Khrushchev therefore took measures to discredit Stalin's name by focusing on the man's brutality and many personal deficiencies.*

From *Stalin and the Soviet Union* by Stephen J. Lee, 1999

Although the contents of Khrushchev's speech were supposed to be secret, illicit copies were soon available and the details flashed around the world. Although some delegates called for the immediate punishment of those involved in Stalin's crimes, not all were impressed by Khrushchev's disclosures and some thought he had gone too far.

Across the country there was an immediate reaction to a speech in which Stalin 'the devoted father of the Russian people' was revealed as a bloodthirsty and criminal tyrant responsible for the deaths of thousands of innocent people. In some of the *gulags* there were riots and thousands appealed claiming that they had been wrongly convicted and imprisoned. At the same time, the process of de-Stalinization began with the dismantling of evidence of the former dictator's tyranny.

De-Stalinization

Of course, millions of Russians already knew the truth about Stalin since they had either been victims or relatives and friends of victims who had suffered under his rule. These, together with the thousands released from the labour camps, reacted strongly against Stalin and Stalinism. Statues and portraits of the former dictator were pulled down and towns and cities that had earlier glorified in his name were given new titles. The heroic city of Stalingrad became Volgagrad, Stalinsk became Novokuznetsk whilst Stalino and Stalinabad changed to Donetsk and Dushanbe respectively. Stalin's body was removed from its place of honour next to Lenin in the Red Square mausoleum to be cremated and his ashes were placed in the wall of the Kremlin behind the tomb. However, it should be mentioned that there are Russians who even now look back on the Stalinist era with nostalgia since it represented a time when hard-pressed workers enjoyed self-respect and appeared to have a purpose in life. Many former Red Army soldiers also recall his brave leadership and remain proud to have served under him, their generalissimo, during the Second World War. What then did Stalin do for Russia? In assessing the achievements of any historical figure there will be pros and cons to consider, and this is certainly true of Josif Stalin. In just ten years, he turned Russia from a backward largely agricultural country into a major industrial nation second only in the world to the United States. In Britain, the same period of change, the Industrial Revolution, took 100 years! This must rate as Stalin's greatest achievement but even so and in spite of spiralling production figures, Russian industry was plagued by wastage, inefficiency and incompetence. Stalin turned an outdated agricultural system into one based on collectivization but the harvests of the collective farms never overtook those of tsarist times. It can be claimed that he provided the Soviet Union with stable government and that during the 34 years of his rule there were no major political upheavals but in order to achieve this he had to use terror and impose an extremely harsh police state-type regime on his people. After the German invasion of Russia in 1941, Stalin led and organized the military and economic needs of the country so that eventually the Red Army was able to defeat the country's invaders but if he had heeded the warnings given him, Russia would have been prepared for war in the first place. Certainly by 1953, Russian standards of living had improved but the betterment was marginal and the standards remained far lower than those in the West. True there were improved educational opportunities but these were not available to all. Is this then a true picture and does it take into consideration the real cost?

In fact, the cost in lives was huge with up to 20 million slaughtered – the kulaks who were murdered and driven from their lands, the Ukrainians who were systematically starved to death, the victims of the purges who were shot or sent to the camps and destined to die from maltreatment. In the end, any final judgement of Stalin's rule must depend on the answer to the moral question 'Does the end justify the means?' Stalin thought it did!

Stalin – some contrasting views

In his book *The Stalin Era*, the historian, Philip Boobbyer, gives us a balanced view of the former Soviet leader:

> *He (Stalin) was a man with definite Marxist-Leninist convictions, and he justified his dictatorship on the grounds that it was necessary. Yet that was not the only thing that drove him. His personality itself seems to have been characterized by a constant and radical mistrust of the world. His policies carried the imprint of this, and as in a Shakespearean tragedy, his own flaws and frustrations were projected onto society at large.*

From *The Stalin Era* by Philip Boobbyer, 2000

However, two views could not be more contradictory than those of Jawaharlal Nehru, the first Indian prime minister, and the Yugoslav dissident, Milovan Djilas:

> *Stalin...that great lover of peace, a man of giant stature who moulded, as few other men have done, the destinies of his age... The occasion is not merely the passing away of a great figure but perhaps the ending of an historic era.*
>
> Jawaharlal Nehru's obituary tribute to Stalin, March 1953

> *Every crime was possible for Stalin and there was not one he had not committed. Whatever standards we use to take his measure, he has the glory of being the greatest criminal in history and, let us hope, for all time to come... If we take the point of view of humanity and as cynical as Stalin was, he was methodical, all embracing, and total as a criminal. He was one of those rare and terrible dogmatists capable of destroying nine-tenths of the human race to make happy the remaining tenth.*
>
> From *Conversations With Stalin* by Milovan Djilas, 1956

Let his biographer, Elizabeth Mauchline Roberts, have the last word:

> *...Stalin has often been compared with Hitler and indeed both claimed millions of victims. But monstrous as were Stalin's crimes, the comparison is unfair to him. Hitler left nothing in Germany but devastation, graves and degradation. Germany made no advance under his rule; in many ways she went backwards along the path of progress, losing most of her claims to be a civilized nation. On the other hand, Stalin, finding the USSR a starving, destitute land, with only the sketchiest foundations for the new Soviet Union, built a powerful industrial state...sharing with the USA the position of the most important state in the world.*
>
> From *Stalin: Man of Steel* by Elizabeth Mauchline Roberts, 1968

Appendix 1

The Republics of the former Soviet Union

Soviet Republic	Now known as	Capital	Population (1995)	Area (sq km)
Armenian SSR	Armenia	Yerevan	3,557,000	29,795
Azerbaijan SSR	Azerbaijan	Baky (Baku)	7,790,000	86,579
Byelorussian SSR	Belarus	Minsk	10,437,000	207,600
Estonian SSR	Estonia	Tallinn	1,625,000	45,100
Georgian SSR	Georgia	Tbilisi	5,726,000	69,700
Kazakh SSR	Kazakhstan	Astana	13,377,000	2,719,500
Kirghiz SSR	Kyrgystan	Bishkek	4,574,000	198,400
Latvian SSR	Latvia	Riga	2,749,000	63,688
Lithuanian SSR	Lithuania	Vilnius	3,876,000	65,201
Moldavian SSR	Moldova	Chisinau	4,490,000	33,670
Russian SFSR	Russia	Moscow	149,909,000	17,070,949
Tadzhik SSR	Tajikistan	Dushanbe	6,155,000	143,100
Turkmen SSR	Turkmenistan	Ashgabat	4,075,000	488,100
Ukrainian SSR	Ukraine	Kiev	51,867,000	601,000
Uzbek SSR	Uzbekistan	Tashkent	23,089,000	449,500

Appendix 2

The coat of arms of the Soviet Union

The centre of the coat of arms of the Soviet Union has a hammer and sickle imposed on a map of the world. It is draped with two bundles of corn and beneath in 15 different languages is the slogan 'Workers of the world unite'.

The national anthem of the Soviet Union

Unbreakable Union of freeborn Republics,
Great Russia has welded forever to stand.
Created in struggle by will of the people,
United and mighty, our Soviet land!

Through tempests the sunrays of freedom have cheered us,
Along the new path where Lenin did lead,
Be true to the people, thus Stalin has reared us,
Inspire us to labour and valorous deed.

In the victory of Communism's deathless ideal,
We see the future of our dear land.

And to the fluttering scarlet banner,
Selflessly true we always shall stand.

Chorus sung after each verse:
Sing to the Motherland, home of the free,
Bulwark of peoples in brotherhood strong,
Party of Lenin, the strength of the people,
To Communism's triumph lead us on.

Glossary

abstract artists Artists who present their work other than in the way it appears to the eye – in geometric or other designs.

anti-clerica l Opposed to the clergy and the power of the clergy.

anti-Semitism A dislike or hatred of the Jews.

atheism Disbelief in the existence of God.

autonomous Guided by the principle of self-government.

black-marketeering Illegally selling scarce or rationed goods at exorbitant prices.

bonus incentives Paying additional wages for increased output by workers.

bourgeoisie The middle class.

centralized bureaucracy Government controlled from the centre in order to have greater control.

Consumer goods Manufactured goods available for customers to buy in shops as distinct from capital goods that are made to be used in the manufacture of other goods.

coup Abbreviated form of *coup d'etat*. The use of violence to overthrow the government of a country.

cult of personality The development of the excessive adulation of a person.

demotic Relating to the people.

elitist Belonging to a select group.

feudalism The organization of society in the Middle Ages when all land was owned by the lords and allocated to peasants in return for part of the crop, payment of a tax or military service.

gulags A system of labour camps in the Soviet Union.

mausoleum A large and elegant tomb.

mobilization Preparing a nation's armed forces for war.

monolith Massive construction resembling a large stone or column.

mystic Mysterious, secret or having some hidden meaning.

nepotism Undue patronage to one's family; giving important positions to members of one's family.

parasitical Living at the expense of others; being a hanger-on.

pince-nez spectacles Spectacles attached to the nose by a spring.

plagiarize To copy the writing of another.

proletariat The wage-earning working class.

protection racket Demanding money in return for leaving people or their property unharmed.

sadism Pleasure gained from inflicting pain on others.

yes-men Obedient followers; people who agree with everything said to them.

zemstvo(s) Administrative unit(s) of local government.

Taking it further

Suggestions for further reading

Last of the Tsars, Richard Tames (Pan Books, 1972)

Life and Terror in Stalin's Russia, Robert W. Thurston (Yale University Press, 1996)

One Day in the Life of Ivan Denisovich, Aleksandr Solzhenitsyn (Collins, 1962)

Religion in the Soviet Union, W. Kolarz (Macmillan, 1961)

Russia 1914–1941, John Laver (Hodder & Stoughton, 1991)

Russia 1917–1945, Clare Baker (Heinemann, 1990)

Russia in Revolution, John L. Taylor (Holmes McDougall, 1974)

Russia Since 1914, Martin McCauley (Longman, 1998)

Russia Under Stalin, J. F. Aylett (Edward Arnold 1984)

Soviet Politics 1945–53, T. Dunmore (Macmillan, 1984)

Stalin, Harold Shukman (Sutton, 1999)

Stalin, Edvard Radzinsky (Sceptre, 1996)

Stalin and Stalinism, Martin McCauley (Longman, 1983)

Stalin and Stalinism, Alan Wood (Routledge, 1990)

Stalin and the Soviet Union, Stephen J. Lee (Routledge, 1999)

Stalin: Man of Steel, Elizabeth Mauchline Roberts (Methuen, 1968)

Stalin's Russia, Martyn Whittock (Collins, 1997)

Stalingrad, Anthony Beevor (Penguin Books, 1998)

The Doctors' Plot, I. Rapoport (Fourth Estate, 1991)

The Making of Modern Russia, Lionel Kochan (Penguin Books, 1962)

The Great Terror, R. Conquest (Penguin Books, 1971)

The Gulag Archipelago, Aleksandr Solzhenitsyn (Collins, 1988)

The Lysenko Affair, D. Joravsk (Harvard University Press, 1970)

The Rise and Fall of the Soviet Empire, Dmitri Volkogonov (HarperCollins, 1999)

The Russian Revolution, Beryl Williams (Blackwell, 1987)

The Siege of Leningrad, C. A. Stanford (Stanford University Press, 1962)

The Soviet Union Since 1917, Martin McCauley (Longman, 1981)

The Stalin Era, Philip Boobbyer (Routledge, 2000)

The USSR 1945–1990, John Laver (Hodder & Stoughton, 1991)

Trotsky, Francis Wyndnam and David King (Penguin Books, 1972)

Victims of Yalta, Nikolai Tolstoy (Corgi Books, 1978)

Vlasov and the Russian Liberation Movement, C. Andreyev (Cambridge University Press, 1987)

Years of Russia and the USSR, David Evans and Jane Jenkins (Hodder & Stoughton, 2001)

20 Letters to a Friend, Svetlana Alliluyeva (World Books, 1967)

Index

Credits

BP 4.12